THE SHAW MEMORIAL

SIDE ELEVATION.

A CELEBRATION OF
AN AMERICAN MASTERPIECE

PROGRAM
FOR THE UNVEILING OF THE SHAW MEMORIAL

PRELUDE MUSIC
Constitution Brass Quintet

INVOCATION
The Reverend Claudia Highbaugh

WELCOME

BYRON BELL
President, Saint-Gaudens Memorial

PRESENTATION OF COLORS
Co. A, 54th Massachusetts Regimental Reenactors
The National Anthem
(The 1865 arrangement by Claudio R. Grafulla/R Edwards)Royal)

JOHN H. DRYFHOUT
Superintendent, Saint-Gaudens National Historic Site

MARIE RUST
Regional Director, Northeast Region, National Park Service

MUSIC OF THE 54TH REGIMENT
We are Coming Father Abraham by Luther O. Emerson
Hoist Up the Flag by Billy Holmes
arranged by Cornell

∾

PROFESSOR VINCENT SCULLY

∾

Shenandoah
Just Before the Battle Mother
Lorena & Bright Smiles

∾

THE HON. WILLIAM T. COLEMAN, JR.

∾

Battle Cry of Freedom

REMARKS BY DESCENDANTS OF THE 54TH REGIMENT:
Professor Robert Shaw Oliver Harding
Major George Henry Coblyn, U.S. Army, Retired

∾

Maggie By My Side Grand March
Yankee Doodle
Dixie & The Bonnie Blue Flag

THE UNVEILING OF THE SHAW MEMORIAL
at the monument in the garden

The Cornish Elementary School Children's Chorus, Director Molly Bonhag
Lift Every Voice
Battle Hymn of the Republic

Acceptance of the sculpture by the National Park Service

∾

Refreshments in the tent following the unveiling

You are invited to view the exhibition:
The Shaw Memorial: A Celebration of An American Masterpiece
in the Picture Gallery

Constitution Brass Quintet
JoAnne Edwards, cornet
David Heintz, cornet
Christina Otten, horn
Ben Edwards, trombone
William Keck, tuba
D. Thomas Toner, drums

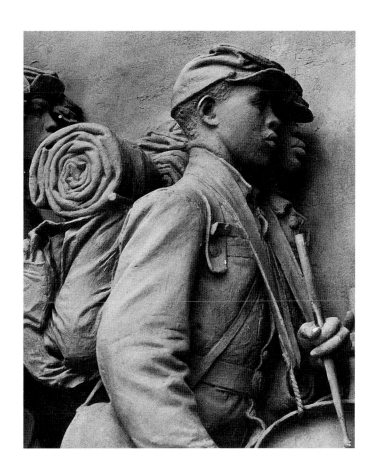

FROM THE PRESIDENT OF THE SAINT-GAUDENS MEMORIAL

The Trustees of the Saint-Gaudens Memorial are honored to have played a major role in this historic project to conserve and cast the final version of Saint-Gaudens' magnificent Shaw Memorial. This has been a project of huge dimension; not just in terms of the physical size of the work, but with regard to the complexity of the undertaking and its import, which extends far beyond the bounds of the Historic Site. The plaster cast has been preserved and will be unveiled at the National Gallery of Art, Washington, D.C. in September. The bronze, which will be unveiled on July 13, will stand in the open air at Saint-Gaudens' former home and studios, and will continue in perpetuity the presence here of one of Saint-Gaudens' most important works. These events are the result of many people working in concert to perpetuate the extraordinary art and vision of one of America's greatest artists.

This project is part of a long tradition of ventures and activities undertaken by the Trustees since 1919 to increase public knowledge and appreciation of Saint-Gaudens' work. Among those ventures have been the casting of two other major works for the Site: the Adams Memorial and the Farragut Monument.

Also a tradition, since the creation of the Saint-Gaudens National Historic Site in 1965, is our on-going collaboration with the National Park Service and, increasingly, with the local communities. This magnificent historic site thrives in large part because the Trustees, the federal government, and the communities have worked together to ensure that the priceless artistic, architectural and natural resources at the site are preserved while allowing for needed changes and development.

Many talented people have helped to carry on this tradition of collaboration, most notably my able predecessors, former Memorial presidents Charles A. Platt, John R. Gilman, and Kent L. Barwick, and the distinguished Superintendent of the Site, John H. Dryfhout. Their efforts, along with those of other Trustees, community leaders, and National Park Service staff, have greatly benefitted the Site, and laid the groundwork for preservation and appropriate improvements to continue into the future, through the recently approved General Management Plan.

We are immensely grateful to all of the individuals who have worked on and contributed to the Shaw project, but I would like to single out a few for special thanks:

Thank you to all the Trustees of the Saint-Gaudens Memorial, every one of whom supported this project with their contributions and enthusiasm; and, in particular, Mr. & Mrs. David F. Putnam, Mary Kaplan and The J.M. Kaplan Fund, and Mr. & Mrs. Richard J. Schwartz, whose continued and expansive generosity have made this and other important projects possible.

Thank you to John Dryfhout, Superintendent of the Saint-Gaudens National Historic Site, an authority on the work of Saint-Gaudens, who from the outset worked with energy and dedication, first to make this project possible and then to ensure that every element of the endeavor was approached and completed properly and held to the highest standard of excellence.

Thank you to the Trustees who gave so generously of their time and expertise to make this project a success: specifically Vice President Frank C. Platt; Shaw Project Co-Chairs Ellen Rublee and Jock Reynolds; architect Daniel V. Scully, landscape architect Alan Saucier; and sculptor Robert W. White.

Thank you to all the dedicated individuals from the National Park Service who contributed to this great effort, including Marie Rust, NE Regional Director and Robert McIntosh, NE Region Associate Director; at the Saint-Gaudens National Historic Site, Gregory C. Schwarz, Chief of Interpretation; Ross Houghton, Acting Facility Manager; Martha G. Knapp, Conservation Specialist; April May Gelineau, Administrative Technician; and James Haaf, Chief Gardener; Brigid Sullivan and Carol Warner, Conservators from the NE Region's Cultural Resource Center; and John Maounis, NE Region Curator.

Also thank you to the contractors, who brought their experience, professionalism and patience to this project: Clifford Craine of Daedalus, Inc., Cambridge, MA (plaster conservation); Robert Shure of Skylight Studios, Woburn, MA (molding and project oversight): Robert and Jeffrey Spring of Modern Art Foundry, Long Island City, NY (casting); and Neil R. Ackley of The MacMillin Company, Keene, NH (base construction).

We look forward to future projects that will enhance the Saint-Gaudens Site and keep alive the artistic tradition of Augustus Saint-Gaudens

Byron Bell
President of the Board of Trustees

THE SHAW MEMORIAL PROJECT COMMITTEE

THE CAMPAIGN FOR THE SHAW MEMORIAL

The Saint-Gaudens Memorial, the National Park Service and the National Gallery of Art, Washington, D.C., have collaborated on a project to preserve, restore and recast the heroic size plaster Shaw Memorial, Saint Gaudens' final version of his magnificent tribute to the men of the Fifty-Fourth Massachusetts Regiment and their colonel, Robert Gould Shaw.

Thank you to the following individuals, whose contrbutions made possible the creation of a new bronze cast of the Shaw Memorial for permanent installation at the Saint-Gaudens National Historic Site in Cornish, New Hampshire:

Dr. F. H. Ahrens
James B. Atkinson
The Badger Fund, NHCF
Kent L. Barwick
Tom & Ann Barwick
Byron & Susan Bell
Laura H. Belman
Max Blumberg & Eduardo Araujo
Terry Bonneville
Matthew Broderick
Alice C. Brown
James & Judy Brown
Dr. & Mrs. Robert E. Carroll
The Chace Fund
Malcom G. Chace III & Eliot Nolen
Ivan Chermayeff
Hon. & Mrs. William T. Coleman
M. Lynn Conover & Gregory W. Peach
Gary DesGroseilliers & Katrina I. Csigi
Char Delabar
John H. Dryfhout
Mrs. Federick Eaton
Mrs. G. D'Arcy Edmondson
Francis F. Faulkner
Philip & Patricia Faulkner
Natalie & Raymond Feldman
Gilbert Franklin
Frank & Joseph Gallo, Editions in Cast Paper Ltd.
Francis Gilbert
John & Julie Gilman

Josephine Goodden
Robert F. Gordon
Kathryn Greenthal
Agnes Gund
Robert S. O. Harding
Francis W. & Serenia M. Hatch
Fenno & Carol Heath Jr.
Roger W. Hooker, Jr.
Ms. Lena Horne
Milton & Miriam Hurwitz
Mrs. Sally Iselin
Ann & Carol Jacobs
Mary Kaplan
Mary J. Karraker
Ellen S. Kean
Malcolm R. Kent
Grace F. Knowlton
Winston Kulok
Henry & Joan Lee
Mrs. Barbara Lewis
Neil MacNeil
Mrs. Francis W. MacVeagh
Glenn R. Mairo
Markem Corporation
MacDonald Mathey
Berri T. McBride
Joseph & Anne McCann
Mary Goodyear Mckee
The MacMillin Company
Paul Moravec & Wendy Lamb
National Park Service
Mr. & Mrs. Anthony Neidecker
William and Nelly Palmer
Mr. & Mrs. Richard D. Parsons

The Joan Whitney & Charles Shipman Payson Foundation
PepsiCo Foundation
Arthur Platt
Charles & Joan Platt
Frank & Judy Platt
Tim Prentice
The Putnam Foundation
Mr. & Mrs. David F. Putnam
James & Judith Putnam
Regal Construction
Jock Reynolds
Frederick P. & Sandra P. Rose Foundation
Arthur Ross Foundation
Ellen & George Rublee
Alan Saucier
Hanna Schad
Richard J. Schwartz
Mr. & Mrs. Howard C. Sherman
Charles Shurcliff
Caroline Storrs
Susan E. Strickler
Charles & Barbara Tarbox
Douglas F. Thompson
Marion Trepanier
Alan T. Wenzell
Burke Wilkinson
Lucia Williams
Alexander & Amy White
Robert & Claire White
Joyce & Walter Wolff
Richard P. Wunder

SGNHS #1436.

SGNHS #1244.

SGNHS #1438.

Studies of heads for use in the Shaw Memorial;
done in one-third lifesize by Augustus Saint-Gaudens,
as he worked on the monument, 1883-1893.
Collection of Saint-Gaudens National Historic Site.

SGNHS #1242.

SGNHS #1437.

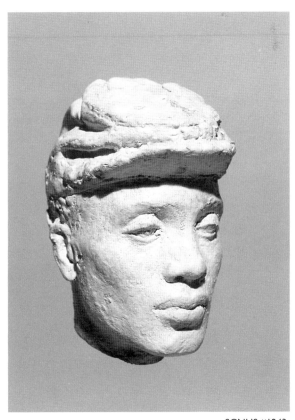

SGNHS #1243.

INSCRIPTIONS ON
THE SHAW MONUMENT IN BOSTON

On the front of the monument, part of the relief itself:

OMNIA RELINQVIT / SERVARE REMPVBLICAM

Underneath the relief:

ROBERT GOULD SHAW

COLONEL·OF·THE·FIFTY·FOURTH·REGIMENT·OF·MASSA-
CHUSETTS·INFANTRY·BORN·IN·BOSTON·10·OCTOBER·
MDCCCXXXVII·KILLED·WHILE·LEADING·THE·ASSAULT·
ON·FORT·WAGNER·
SOUTH·CAROLINA·18·JULY·MDCCCLXIII

Underneath, the verse of James Russel Lowell:

RIGHT·IN·THE·VAN·ON·THE·RED·RAMPART'S·SLIPPERY·
SWELL·WITH·HEART·THAT·BEAT·A·CHARGE·HE·FELL·
FOEWARD·AS·FITS·A·MAN: BUT·THE·HIGH·SOUL·BURNS·
ON·TO·LIGHT·MEN'S·FEET·WHERE·DEATH·FOR·NOBLE·
ENDS·MAKES·DYING·SWEET

On the back of the frame of the tablet.
The inscription was composed by Charles W. Eliot

TO THE FIFTY FOURTH
OF MASSACHUSETTS
REGIMENT INFANTRY

THE WHITE OFFICERS / TAKING LIFE AND HONOR IN
THEIR HANDS CAST IN THEIR LOT WITH MEN OF
A DESPISED RACE UNPROVED IN WAR AND RISKED
DEATH AS INCITERS OF SERVILE INSURRECTION IF
TAKEN PRISONERS BESIDES ENCOUNTERING ALL THE
COMMON PERILS OF CAMP MARCH AND BATTLE

THE BLACK RANK AND FILE VOLUNTEERED WHEN
DISASTER CLOUDED THE UNION CAUSE SERVED
WITHOUT PAY FOR EIGHTEEN MONTHS TILL GIVEN
THAT OF WHITE TROOPS FACED THREATENED
ENSLAVEMENT IF CAPTURED WERE BRAVE IN ACTION
PATIENT UNDER HEAVY AND DANGEROUS
LABORS AND CHEERFUL AMID
HARDSHIPS AND PRIVATIONS

TOGETHER
THEY GAVE TO THE NATION AND THE WORLD
UNDYING PROOF THAT AMERICANS OF AFRICAN
DESCENT POSSESS THE PRIDE COURAGE
AND DEVOTION OF THE PATRIOT SOLDIER
ONE HUNDRED AND EIGHTY THOUSAND SUCH
AMERICANS ENLISTED UNDER THE UNION FLAG IN
MDCCCLXIII - MDCCCLXV

Underneath on the back. Inscribed in 1897 were the names of the other five officers killed in battle. Of these, only Russel and Simpkins died at Fort Wagner.

CABOT JACKSON RUSSEL   WILLIAM HARRIS SIMPKINS
CAPTAIN   CAPTAIN

EDWARD LEWIS STEVENS   DAVID REID
1ST LIEUTENANT   1ST LIEUTENANT

FREDERICK HEDGE WEBSTER
2ND LIEUTENANT

Underneath these names is an extract from the address given by Governor Andrew on the departure of the regiment:

I KNOW NOT MR COMMANDER WHERE
IN ALL HUMAN HISTORY TO ANY
GIVEN THOUSAND MEN IN ARMS THERE
HAS BEEN COMMITTED A WORK AT
ONCE SO PROUD SO PRECIOUS SO FULL OF
HOPE AND GLORY AS THE
WORK COMMITTED TO YOU

On the marble at one end of the terrace, words of Mrs. Waterston:

O FAIR HAIRED NORTHERN HERO WITH
THY GUARD OF DUSKY HUE
UP FROM THE FIELD OF BATTLE RISE
TO THE LAST REVIEW

On the marble at the other end of the terrace the words of Ralph Waldo Emerson:

STAINLESS SOLDIER ON THE WALLS
KNOWING THIS AND KNOWS NO MORE
WHOEVER FIGHTS WHOEVER FALLS
JUSTICE CONQUERS EVERMORE

In 1981, the names of the following enlisted men of the Fifty-Fourth killed in action during the war, were added to the monument. These names did not include those who died of their wounds, died in prison camps, died of disease, or were listed as missing after battle. A complete roster of the Fifty-Fourth Regiment may be found in *History of the Fifty-Fourth Regiment of Massachusetts Volunteer Infantry,* 1863-1865, by Capt. Luis Emilio.

Henry Albert
Thomas R. Ampey
Thomas Bowman
William Brady
Abraham Brown
James H. Buchanan
Henry F. Burghardt
Elisha Burkett
Jason Champlin
Andrew Clark
Lewis Clark
Henry Craig
Josephus Curry
Edward Darks
Henry Dennis
William Edgerly
Albert Evans
William S. Everson
Samuel Ford
Richard M. Foster
Charles S. Gamrell

Lewis C. Green
John Hall
William Henry Harrison, 2nd
Edward Hines
Benjamin Hogan
Charles M. Holloway
George Jackson
James P. Johns
John H. Johnson
Daniel A. Kelley
Henry King
Cyrus Krunkleton
Augustus Lewis
Thomas Lloyd
William Lloyd
Lewis J. Locard
Francis Lowe
Robert McJohnson
John Miller
James H. Mills
William H. Morris

Charles E. Nelson
Stephen Newton
Harrison Pierce
Cornelius Price
Thomas Peter Riggs
David R. Roper
Anthony Schenck
Thomas Sheldon
William J. Smith
Samuel Sufshay
John Tanner
William Thomas
Charles Van Allen
George Vanderpool
Cornelius Watson
Edward Williams
Franklin Willis
Joseph D. Wilson
William Wilson
John W. Winslow

CONTENTS

PREFACE

Soon after coming to the Saint-Gaudens National Historic Site it was my good fortune to meet sculptor Leonard Baskin and his friend and colleague Sidney Kaplan. They told me of an earlier visit to Cornish, and finding the beautiful plaster sketches, studies of the heads for the soldiers in the Shaw Memorial. They were so inspired that they urged the Saint-Gaudens Memorial trustees to preserve the sketches by casting them in bronze. Professor Kaplan was completing his research for the 1973 National Portrait Gallery exhibition and catalogue, "The Black Presence in the Era of the American Revolution." He continued this work with "The Black Soldier of the Civil War in Literature and Art" published as the Chancellor's Lecture at the University of Massachusetts, Amherst, in October 1979. He was active in the 1981 fundraising for the restoration of the Boston monument, and finally the 1989 publication of his work on Saint-Gaudens in the *Massachusetts Review.* Sidney is gone now, but his contribution to the literature on Saint-Gaudens and the Shaw Memorial are recalled now as we celebrate this event; not only the centenary of the monument itself, but also the celebration of this great American masterpiece in the unveiling of the bronze cast of this, Saint-Gaudens' final rendition of the monument.

In 1970, our late trustee and Dartmouth College music professor, James Sykes, mounted an exhibition here at Cornish and a presentation of the music of Charles Ives; recalling on piano and in song, Ives' symphonic trilogy: "Three Places in New England," the first of which is entitled, "The Shaw in Boston Common: Moving, Marching Faces of Souls". Ives wrote and composed that piece in the first decade of this century. Ives was not the first artist to have been inspired to creativity based on Saint-Gaudens' masterpiece, as is so well documented in Larry Lauerhass' essay: "The Shaw Memorial, A Consecration," documenting the metamorphosis of the epic in prose, verse, film, video and continuing in the historical reenactment dramatic performances by volunteers in communities throughout the country.

That story of the Fifty-Fourth Massachusetts Regiment is ever worthy of retelling. Gregory Schwarz has given us not only the complete history of the Monument but the history of the Fifty-Fourth Regiment of African American troops in the Civil War; the Battle of Fort Wagner and its importance in American history. Through his study, especially from the writings of a veteran of the regiment, Capt. Luis F. Emilio's *A Brave Black Regiment: History of the Fifty-fourth Regiment of Massachusetts Volunteer Infantry*, as well as the host of other publications on the Fifty-Fourth Regiment; he has given us a full account of the great sacrifice of those who served. We have therefore included those names in the exhibition at the Saint-Gaudens National Historic Site. As General Colin Powell so movingly said in his speech to those gathered in Boston on May 31, 1997, the 100th anniversary of the monument, they are covered "in glory everlasting".

For Saint-Gaudens, the monument was a labor of love. In our commentary on the monument we often say he worked on the sculpture for fourteen years before it was unveiled in Boston in 1897. We now know that Saint-Gaudens worked on this masterpiece an additional three years, and the bronze cast that we unveil here in 1997 is this, the sculptor's final artistic rendition.

We read in the essay by conservator Brigid Sullivan of the almost 100 years of treatment this fragile work has received, and how fortunate indeed that it was protected and cared for in these intervening years. Much of the credit for that goes to the Trustees of the Saint-Gaudens Memorial, who in the 1940s had the foresight and tenacity to acquire and exhibit the monument and to protect it these past fifty years.

Their gift of the bronze preserves not only this final version here for the thousands of visitors who come each year, but it also permits us to make the original plaster available on long-term loan to the National Gallery of Art in Washington, D.C., where it will be viewed by many thousands of visitors each year and protected under proper museum environmental conditions.

This particular joint effort of the Saint-Gaudens Memorial Trustees and the National Park Service, began following the Trustees' annual meeting in July 1995, when the Shaw Memorial fund raising effort was initiated. In March 1996, the proposal by the National Gallery of Art for conservation together with the long term loan and exhibition of the original plaster was accepted and the agreement signed by then National Park Service Director Roger Kennedy and Regional Director Marie Rust.

We are indeed fortunate to have such a group of friends, and a partnership that has been in place for more than thirty years since the National Park Service was given these properties by the Trustees of the Memorial in 1965. Their efforts over the years, sustained the place and assured that this would be the first artist's home and studio to be preserved and protected in the National Park system and what is more, provided us a collection of some of the finest art works that this great sculptor produced.

I would like to take this opportunity to thank Byron Bell, President of the Memorial and the officers, trustees and donors who have brought this project to such a successful completion.

In addition to those individuals already mentioned in other parts of the catalogue and program, I would like to especially thank Barbara Homeyer, for her design and production of the catalogue.

The exhibition and this catalogue were made possible by a substantial gift of Mr. and Mrs. David Putnam together with the Saint-Gaudens Memorial trustees and a grant from the Eastern National Park & Monument Association.

John H. Dryfhout
Superintendent

THE
FIFTY-FOURTH
REGIMENT

The Massachusetts Fifty-Fourth Regiment was the first military unit raised in the North of "persons of African descent." Though not the first Union military unit made up of African Americans, it was the most famous of such regiments during the Civil War, and remains so today. It was the brave conduct of this Regiment during the attack on Fort Wagner, South Carolina, in July 1863, that inspired widespread enlistment of blacks into the Union forces.

Though early in the war, white abolitionists joined black leaders like Frederick Douglass, in calling for the enlistment of African Americans into the army, there was widespread prejudice in the North against taking this step. Despite the fact that blacks served with American forces during the Revolution, many whites believed that the blacks would fight poorly, if at all, and were also incapable of learning military discipline. Even President Lincoln was hesitant to officially approve this measure.

With the signing of the Emancipation Proclamation on January 1, 1863, Congress reluctantly authorized the raising of regiments composed of African Americans, and only then if the officers were white. Governor John A. Andrew of Massachusetts was one of the first to raise such a regiment. Andrew was an abolitionist and an early supporter of enlistment of blacks.

When Governor Andrew looked for a colonel to head the new regiment, he immediately thought of Robert Gould Shaw, son of George Shaw and Sarah Blake (Sturgis) Shaw, a prominent Bostonian family.

Col. Robert Gould Shaw (1837-1863).
Courtesy U.S. Military History Institute.

The Shaws were also staunch abolitionists, and strongly supported the formation of an African American regiment. After being contacted by Governor Andrew, Shaw's father at once sent word to his son, then on duty with the Massachusetts Second Regiment in Virginia.

Born in Boston on October 10, 1837, Robert Gould Shaw had studied and traveled in Europe as a young man. After his return to the United States, he enrolled at Harvard University, withdrawing in his junior year to work for his uncle, Henry P. Sturgis, who had a business in New York City. Shaw soon found that he disliked the work, and on April 19, 1861, answering President Lincoln's call for troops, enlisted in the Seventh New York Regiment. His regiment was sent to Virginia, but Shaw saw no action during his short time with them.

On May 28, 1861, Shaw received a commission as second lieutenant in the Massachusetts Second Regiment. By July 8, 1861, he was made first lieutenant, and on August 10, 1862, was promoted to Captain. During his service with the Second Massachusetts, he saw his first combat, fighting in some small skirmishes and the battles of Cedar Mountain and Antietam, where he was wounded in the neck. At one skirmish he was spared a mortal wound when his gold pocket watch stopped a bullet.[1]

Shaw's first reaction upon receiving Governor Andrew's offer of command of the Fifty-Fourth, was to refuse. He preferred to stay with his regiment where he had friends, and felt confident of rapid advancement. Shaw also knew that this African American regiment was an important experiment, and had reservations about his being the best man for the post. He wrote a letter declining the offer, but the very next day, reconsidered and decided to accept. Shaw felt it might be cowardly of him to refuse, and he also did not want to disappoint his parents.

The formation of a black regiment met with indignation in the south. The Confederate Congress issued a proclamation that any African Americans captured in uniform would be sold into slavery. White officers of such regiments would be considered as inciting servile insurrection and executed. While this was never put into practice with captured Union troops, at the time it was a very real and serious consideration for black and white soldiers alike, and was an especially troublesome thought to those soldiers who were once slaves.

Recruiting began in Boston on February 9, 1863, and by February 21, barracks were established at Camp Meigs, in Readville, Massachusetts, outside of Boston. It soon became apparent that there would not be enough enlistments from Massachusetts alone to quickly fill the regiment. Recruitment was therefore begun elsewhere including New York, Indiana, Missouri, Ohio, and even Canada. Later, these states would form their own regiments of African American volunteers, but at the time the idea was untested, and recruiters met with widespread prejudice against enlistment of blacks. In some instances, in order to avoid trouble, new recruits were sent off to the camp in Readville in small groups under cover of darkness.

Training began in earnest as soon as the first recruits arrived. Shaw, at first dubious about the abilities of the recruits, soon found them responding well to military discipline. He even commented that they were better in this respect than the Irish troops with whom he had experience in other regiments.

Recruiting poster, 1863. Courtesy Massachusetts Historical Society.

By May 12, 1863, the regiment finally reached its full strength of 1,000 men, and consisted of companies A-I, and K. The men had been issued standard infantry uniforms of light blue. Shaw had insisted that they not be issued the darker blue uniform then used by orderlies and blacks working for the army. The troops also received the .577 cal. Enfield rifled muskets. Imported from England, these were used in great numbers by both sides in the war.

On May 18, 1863, Governor Andrew presented the Regiment with its colors. Four flags were received; a national flag, the Massachusetts state flag, a regimental standard of white silk with the figure of the Goddess of Liberty, and the motto "Liberty, Loyalty, and Unity," and another flag with a cross upon a blue field, and the motto, *In Hoc Signo Vinces* (In this sign, victory).

Soon thereafter, a private in Company A, was inspired to write the song "Hoist the Flag," with the chorus:

Oh! give us a flag all free without a slave,
We'll fight to defend it as our fathers did so brave.
The gallant Comp'ny A will make the rebels dance;
And we'll stand by the Union, if we only have a chance.[2]

Also on May 18, a request came from General David Hunter, commanding the Department of the South, asking for Shaw's regiment to proceed to Beaufort, South Carolina. Ten days later, on the morning of May 28, 1863, the regiment broke camp and made a grand march through Boston. Colonel Shaw rode at the head of his troops, and as they passed his parent's home at 44 Beacon Street, he turned to his family gathered on the balcony and raised his sword to his lips. Along with his parents and sisters, stood his wife of three weeks, Anne Kneeland Haggerty.

Also watching the troops was the famous orator, and black leader, Frederick Douglass. Early in the war, Douglass had spoken widely on the idea that African Americans should be allowed to enlist in the army to fight for the Union. His sons, Lewis and Charles, joined the regiment when it was formed, and both would survive the war.

The reception from the populace was one of encouragement and excitement. Crowds lined the streets, but there were no obvious incidents of disrespect. Unbeknownst to most onlookers, however, additional police were kept in reserve out of sight in case of trouble. During the march, the regiment passed in front of the State House where

Governor Andrew waited with his staff, past the very spot where thirty-four years later the Memorial would stand. As the regiment continued on its way to the harbor, the band struck up the popular tune *John Brown's Body*.

Among the onlookers in Boston that morning, was the abolitionist and pacifist poet, John Greenleaf Whittier. Throughout the war he steadfastly refused to look at any troops, or write verse that in any way would contribute to armed conflict. He did, however, watch the Fifty-Fourth that day, and later wrote: "The only regiment I ever looked upon during the war was the Fifty-Fourth Massachusetts on its departure for the South. I can never forget the scene as Colonel Shaw rode at the head of his men. The very flower of grace and chivalry, he seemed to me beautiful and awful, as an angel of God come down to lead the host of freedom to victory."[3]

The regiment embarked on the new transport, *De Molay*, arriving on Hilton Head Island, South Carolina, on June 3, 1863. Here they came under the overall command of Major General David Hunter. An enthusiastic proponent of black troops, in 1862, Hunter formed the First Regiment of South Carolina Volunteers from among runaway and freed slaves.

Frederick Douglass (1817-1895)

Unlike the volunteers recruited for the Fifty-Fourth, not all of Hunter's men joined willingly. Some Union officers later commented that this was a good example of how not to go about enlisting African American troops. Hunter's first black regiment was soon disavowed by the government, though he was later given permission to proceed with his venture, and had reorganized this unit by the time the Fifty-Fourth arrived. Also by May, 1863, Hunter's subordinate, Colonel James Montgomery, had formed another black Regiment, The Second South Carolina Volunteers.

On June 10, Montgomery asked for Shaw's troops to accompany his regiment on a foraging expedition inland to Darien, Georgia. Shaw was excited to have his men participate in this raid, their first action against the enemy, but soon found that Montgomery's primary aim appeared to be looting. Darien was a small, pleasant town of no military value, and the few enemy troops had withdrawn. After looting the town, Montgomery ordered the buildings set afire. Shaw protested the burning, but he and his men had to concede to direct orders. Only one company of the Fifty-Fourth participated in setting the fires.

On July 6, Shaw wrote to General Strong, requesting transfer of the Fifty-Fourth to his command and a more active theater. He suggested that it was important to have black troops be associated with white soldiers as much as possible, so there would be other witnesses to their capabilities. General Strong complied and on July 8, the regiment was transferred to James Island, South Carolina under Strong's command.

It was on James Island that the regiment received its first taste of combat. On July 16, while manning a picket line, they were attacked by a superior number of Confederate troops intent on recapturing the island. The Fifty-Fourth stubbornly held the line in hand

The bombproof at Fort Wagner that protected the garrison during the artillery bombardment. Photograph taken after occupation by Union forces. Courtesy U.S. Military History Institute.

to hand fighting until they were able to withdraw in good order. The Regiment's brave stand allowed three companies of the Tenth Connecticut, stationed in a precarious position, to escape certain destruction or capture. Their bravery, though, came at a price of eleven dead, thirteen captured and twenty-four wounded.[4]

The soldiers retired to nearby Morris Island, where strong Confederate gun batteries stood at Fort Wagner, guarding Charleston harbor. Federal troops occupied most of the island, with the objective of taking this fort which was essentially the key to breaking the defense of Charleston. If Wagner was captured, Fort Sumter and other defenses would be open to fire from Union land-based batteries, and could be subdued.

Battery Wagner, as it was called by its defenders, was a massive earthwork fortification, situated on a small peninsula at the northern end of Morris Island. The only land approach was along a narrow spit of land with the ocean on one side and a marsh on the other. The fort's earthworks were said to be the largest ever made to that time. Behind the walls was a "bombproof" of earth and sandbags, which served as a bunker to protect the 1,700 man garrison during artillery bombardment. Armaments included a number of large artillery pieces which could shoot solid shot and canister. The latter consisted of a projectile filled with a mass of small iron balls, 1-2 inches in diameter. When fired it had a shotgun-like effect which could prove devastating to attacking troops.

An attack on Wagner a week earlier, had been repulsed with heavy casualties. General Seymour wanted to make another frontal assault, believing he could capture the fort, though many other officers thought it fruitless. Colonel Shaw was anxious for the chance to prove his men in battle, and when he met with General Strong, asked him to allow the Fifty-Fourth to participate. Shaw's men had virtually no rest and little food for the last two days, but this was the opportunity they had wanted. Strong, aware of the men's situation, replied, "your men, I know, are worn out, but do as you choose."[5]

A heavy artillery bombardment from sea and land batteries hit the fort with an enormous barrage. The shelling, however, proved ineffective against the sandbagged guns and earthworks. When the firing ceased, none of the Confederate cannon were damaged, and the garrison had suffered only eight killed and twenty wounded. Before the Fifty-Fourth began their fateful charge, the full defenses of the fort were ready for them.

Because of sickness, casualties suffered at James Island, and a strong guard left at their camp, only 600 men of the Fifty-Fourth were involved in the battle. They arrived at the Island about 3:00 P.M. and marched to within 1,000 yards of Fort Wagner where they waited. Besides the Fifty-Fourth in the first wave, were white troops from Connecticut, New York and New Hampshire regiments that were to follow in a second wave.

At 7:45 P.M., when it was almost dark, Shaw gave the command to advance. One officer later remembered that Shaw told the men "I want you to prove yourselves . . . The eyes of thousands will look on what you do tonight."[6] When they were within a hundred yards of the fort, Shaw ordered the charge. He had instructed the men not to shoot during the advance, but to only attack with bayonets. As the soldiers ran toward the fort they were met with a withering fire from musket and cannon. Men fell wounded or dead with each enemy volley, but the regiment pressed on, climbing through a ditch and up the sloping walls of the fort.

Shaw at the head of his men, mounted the top of the parapet with his sword in the air and shouted "forward Fifty-Fourth."[7] At that very moment he toppled forward, shot in the chest. Others also made it to the top of the wall, including the standard bearer. He too was hit, but as he fell Sergeant William Carney grabbed the flag. Though wounded in the chest and arms, Carney eventually made it back into camp late that night. Still holding the tattered flag, he entered the field hospital tent and remarked to his comrades " I never let the dear old flag touch the ground boys."[8] Carney was later awarded the Congressional Medal of Honor for his actions, the first African American so honored.

The nurse, Clara Barton, who later founded the American Red Cross, watched the battle from the Union flagship, "I saw the bayonets glisten . . . and the dark line of blue trailed into the belching walls of Wagner. I saw them on, up and over the parapets into the jaws of death, and

Sgt. William H. Carney holding the flag he saved at Fort Wagner.
Courtesy U.S. Military History Institute.

Storming Fort Wagner. Chromolithograph by Kurz & Allison (Chicago, 1890).

heard the clang of the death-dealing sabers as they grappled with the foe. I saw . . . the wounded, slowly crawling to me down the tide-washed beach."[9] Praise even came from a Confederate lieutenant, Iredell Jones, "The Negroes fought gallantly, and were headed by as brave a colonel as ever lived. He mounted the breastworks waving his sword, at the head of his regiment, and he and an orderly sergeant fell dead over the inner crest of the works."[10]

Harriet Tubman, black Union scout, and famed 'conductor' for the "underground railway," also witnessed the battle, "And then we saw de lightning, and that was de guns; and then we heard de thunder, and that was de big guns; and then we heard de rain falling, and that was de drops of blood falling; and when we came to get in de crops, it was dead men that we reaped."[11] Tubman later helped nurse the wounded and bury the dead.

The next morning a truce was declared while the dead were buried, though the Confederates refused Union assistance. A Union prisoner Assistant Surgeon, John T. Luck, reported being shown the body of a colonel and an African American sergeant lying side by side. The other white officers that fell were given an honorable burial, but he related that Shaw was stripped of his uniform and thrown into the common grave with the enlisted men. This was intended as an insult because of Shaw's command of black troops. The surgeon later claimed that Brigadier General Hagood had said "I had known Shaw before the war and he was an honorable man. Had he been in command of white troops, I should have given him an honorable burial; as it is, I shall bury him in the common trench with the Negroes that fell with him."[12] After the war Hagood denied having known Shaw, or saying anything like this. Northern papers, however, soon reported the quote as the more inflammatory, "He is buried with his niggers," which aroused indignation in the north and helped the recruiting efforts for new black regiments.

After the battle, the Union commanders changed their tactics, and decided to lay siege to Fort Wagner as well as continue an unrelenting artillery bombardment. Finally, on September 6, the battered fort was abandoned by its defenders, and occupied by Union troops, including the Fifty-Fourth. An effort was then planned to recover Shaw's body for proper burial. When his parents heard of this, they immediately wrote to General Gilmore and requested that their son's body not be disturbed. "We hold that a soldier's most appropriate burial place is on the field where he has fallen."[1] Because of relentless erosion of the sea, much of the fort and the burial site of those slain during the battle is now under water.

Total Union casualties in the battle amounted to 1,515, while the Confederates suffered only 171. Among the Fifty-Fourth, at least nineteen men were captured, and held at prisons in and around Charleston, at least ten of them later died. Forty seven men were listed as missing, many of those probably killed during the attack. Over 149 were wounded in the battle, of whom at least twenty-five died of their wounds. In all, the regiment suffered 281 casualties among the 600 men who fought that day.[13] White troops in the second wave of the assault also endured high casualties including General Strong, who was mortally wounded. Among the New Hampshire troops killed that day was Brigadier General Haldimand S. Putnam, a native of Cornish, N.H.[13] Coincidentally, it was in this small New England town that Saint-Gaudens would later establish a studio and spend the last seven years of his life.

Shortly after the battle, Edward L. Pierce, correspondent for the *New York Daily Tribune*, spoke with the mortally wounded General Strong. Strong's remarks echoed those of many other observers: "The Fifty-fourth did well and nobly . . . They moved up as gallantly as any troops could, and with their enthusiasm they deserved a better fate."[14]

Two other officers of the Fifty-Fourth were killed in the assault and many wounded, including Lt. Col. Edward Hallowell. After his recovery, Hallowell took over command of the regiment, and remained in this position for the remainder of the war.

On February 20, 1864, the regiment joined in a campaign across northern Florida under the command of General Truman Seymour. While marching toward Tampa, they were attacked by a superior Confederate force near Olustee. The battle was a southern victory, but the Fifty-Fourth fought a commendable rear guard action to protect the withdrawal of troops, saving many from certain capture. Again, the unit won praise for their action. Several men of the Fifty-Fourth were captured at the battle and sent to the notorious Andersonville prison. One, Corporal James Henry Gooding, who was to die at Andersonville, wrote numerous letters home during his service for publication in his hometown newspaper, the New Bedford, Massachusetts, *Mercury*. In 1991, these were compiled into a book, *On the Altar of Freedom: A Black Soldier's Civil War Letters From the Front.*

One major issue involving the Fifty-Fourth was the issue of pay. Though the men were promised the standard pay of $13, the government only wanted to pay $10 a month, the wage given to black laborers working for the army. In protest, Shaw and his men refused to take their pay until they were paid the same as the white troops. It was not until June 15, 1864, eleven months after the attack on Fort Wagner, that this issue was finally resolved through an act of Congress. The men were then authorized to receive equal pay to that of white soldiers, and the action was retroactive.

The Fifty-Fourth was involved in two larger battles during the remainder of the war, one at Honey Hill, South Carolina on November 30, 1864, and the last on April 18, 1865, at Boykins Mills, South Carolina, nine days after Robert E. Lee surrendered at Appomattox Courthouse.

On September 1, 1865, final payments were made to the men of the Fifty-Fourth, and the discharge papers distributed. The following day, the regiment landed in Boston where they marched a final time through the streets as they had done over two years before, and where they were once again greeted by cheering crowds. At the State House, they were met by Governor John Andrew, and after a ceremonial return of the flags, and a farewell address by Colonel Hallowell, the regiment was officially disbanded. Thirty two years later some of the veterans would return to this spot to march one last time by the monument to their commander and regiment.

By the end of the war, over 175,000 African American men had enlisted in the army and navy, ten percent of the total armed forces. President Lincoln is said to have remarked that participation of African American men in the service won the war for the Union.

Men of the Fifty-Fourth
1. Sgt. Henry Steward (1840-1863)
2. Henry Monroe (1845-1913)
3. Lt. Peter Vogelsang (1815-1887)
Courtesy Massachusetts Historical Society.

THE SHAW MEMORIAL

The *Shaw Memorial* is one of sculptor Augustus Saint-Gaudens' most celebrated masterpieces, and considered by some to be America's greatest public monument. It is also the sculpture that took him the longest to complete, fourteen years from when he first began sketching his ideas with pencil and clay, until the unveiling on Boston Common in 1897, then another three years reworking elements of the monument until it was finished to his satisfaction. The sculpture's development spanned much of Saint-Gaudens' career, from the time when he first achieved fame in the United States, until he reached the height of his recognition in the world of art, when he was awarded a gold medal at the Paris Exposition in 1900.

Augustus Saint-Gaudens was born March 1, 1848, in Dublin, Ireland, to a French shoemaker and his Irish wife. Six months later, the family emigrated to New York City, where Augustus grew up. After completing school at age thirteen, he apprenticed to a cameo cutter, at the same time taking night classes at the Cooper Union and the National Academy of Design. At nineteen with his apprenticeship completed and his mind set on becoming a sculptor, he traveled to Paris where he studied at the renowned École des Beaux-Arts.

In 1870, he left Paris for Rome where for the next five years, he studied classical art and architecture and worked on his first commissions. Here, he also met an American art student, Augusta Homer, whom he later married. In 1876, he received his first major commission, a monument to Civil War Admiral David Glasgow Farragut. Unveiled in New York in 1881, the work was a tremendous success; its combination of realism and allegory was a departure from previous American sculpture. Saint-Gaudens's fame grew, and during his career he would create public monuments to other Civil War heroes the *General John A. Logan Monument; Lincoln, The Man; Lincoln, Head of State;* and the *Shaw Memorial.*

The origins of the *Shaw Memorial* began shortly after the battle of Fort Wagner, when proposals were made by men of the Fifty-Fourth to erect a memorial to their fallen Colonel. Even though the issue of equal pay had not yet been settled, and they had not yet received their pay, amongst themselves the men raised $2,832. An additional $1,000 was contributed by Thomas Wentworth Higginson's African American Regiment, and another $300 by the black population of Beaufort, South Carolina.[18]

The first thought was to erect a simple monument near Fort Wagner and the burial site on Morris Island. Shaw's father suggested that "The monument, though originated for my son, ought to bear, with his, the names of his brave officers and men, who fell and were buried with him. This would be but simple justice. . . ."[19] Because of local hostility, as well as unstable ground conditions, the monument was never erected, but the funds raised were

Joshua B. Smith (1813-1879)
Courtesy Massachusetts Historical Society.

put to a good cause, and used to found the first free school for African American children in Charleston. The school was named in honor of Shaw.

Shaw became a martyr among northern abolitionists, and in 1864, a bust of him was completed by a young sculptor, Edmonia Lewis (1845-1909), whose father was African American and her mother Native American (Chippewa). Lewis sold numerous plaster casts of the sculpture, the proceeds of which she used to finance a trip to Europe where she studied sculpture. While there, she completed a marble copy of the Shaw bust (now in the collections of the Museum of Afro American History, Boston).

Shaw was also remembered in other ways. The New Bedford post of the Grand Army of the Republic (GAR), a national organization of Union veterans, was named in his honor. Most of the men in "C" Company of the Fifty-Fourth had come from New Bedford, which had the largest settlement of blacks in Massachusetts, second to Boston.

In 1865, after the end of hostilities, another effort was begun in Boston to erect a monument closer to home. An African American businessman, Joshua Benton Smith, was the moving force behind a new call for a memorial to Colonel Shaw. A fugitive slave, he had worked for the Shaw family when the Colonel was a child. By the 1860s, Smith had gone on to establish a successful catering business in Boston, and in 1874, served in the Massachusetts legislature. He, along with others, met with Governor Andrew who readily endorsed the idea for the memorial. A committee of twenty-one prominent Bostonians was formed, including the well known abolitionist senator, Charles Sumner, and drafted a statement of purpose, "The Monument is intended not only to mark the public gratitude to the fallen hero who at a critical moment assumed a perilous responsibility, but also to commemorate that great event wherein he was a leader by which the title of colored men as citizen soldiers was fixed beyond recall."[20]

Senator Sumner soon persuaded the committee to ask his friend, the sculptor William Wetmore Story, then in Italy, to create an equestrian statue of Shaw in relief. Soon after this proposal, both Governor Andrew and Senator Sumner died, which appears to have dampened the committee's initiative. The proposal was shelved for the moment, and the committee's activities languished, neither was the project pushed by the Shaw family. Fund raising continued, however, and by 1876 through contributions and judicious investments, the initial $3,161 entrusted to the treasurer, Edward Atkinson, had grown to over $7,000. That same year a committee to raise additional money was organized, and seven years later they could report that the fund had grown to $16,656.[21]

By the fall of 1881, with funds growing steadily enough to move forward with the project, the committee again sought to secure a sculptor. Augustus Saint-Gaudens (1848-1907) had vaulted onto the American art scene earlier that year with his splendid monument to Civil War Admiral David Glasgow Farragut. Unveiled in New York's Madison Square Park on Memorial Day, 1881, the sculpture had instantly met with wide acclaim. Saint-Gaudens' combination of realism and allegory, was a change from the neo-classical style then common, and the base designed by architect Stanford White, with its *Art Nouveau* style bas relief elements, was unlike anything seen before in this country.

Saint-Gaudens' name was recommended to the committee as a possible sculptor for the monument by Edward Atkinson's neighbor, the architect Henry Hobson Richardson. Atkinson also proposed Richardson as the architectural advisor to the project, a suggestion which was soon approved. When Richardson died five years later, his role was assumed by Saint-Gaudens' friend, Charles Follen McKim (1847-1909), of the well known New York architectural firm of McKim, Mead and White.

Augustus Saint-Gaudens (1848-1907). Age 33.

After some initial correspondence, Saint-Gaudens met with the committee in 1882. As was his custom, Saint-Gaudens refused to submit a proposed model for approval unless he was the chosen artist. Because of an unhappy experience competing for a commission several years earlier, he ever afterwards steadfastly refused to participate in any open competitions for such projects. The committee acquiesced. By June 1882, Saint-Gaudens wrote Atkinson, that as he understood the commission was to be awarded him, he would prepare a model for the committee before signing the contract.[22] By mid-December he had three clay sketches completed and was sending them photographs. For most of the following year, Saint-Gaudens worked on sketches and planning for the Memorial, and as the project became finalized, informed the committee that he would begin work on the monument by early December 1883.[23]

The contract was signed on February 23, 1884, and sent to Saint-Gaudens at his New York studio along with a check for $1,500. For the project, the sculptor would receive a total of $15,000.[24] The sculpture was to be delivered in two years, and as the work was originally conceived as a modest bas-relief, the time frame was not unreasonable.

As a young sculptor, the thirty-six year old Saint-Gaudens looked at this as his chance to do a major equestrian figure. He remarked that "I, like most sculptors at the beginning of their careers, felt that by hook or crook I must do an equestrian statue and that here was my opportunity."[25] His first proposal, as seen in the early pencil and clay sketches, was of an equestrian figure of Shaw. The Shaw family, however, demurred,

Early sketches for the Shaw Memorial, December 1882.
Historic photograph, Saint-Gaudens NHS.

Shaw Memorial plaster sketch, 1883.
Sketch submitted for committee approval.
Collection of Saint-Gaudens NHS #25.

noting that Shaw was only a colonel, nor was he a great commander. They thought an equestrian figure would be presumptuous, and should be reserved for men of the highest rank. In response, Saint-Gaudens mused, "accordingly, in casting about for some manner of reconciling my desire (to do an equestrian) with their ideas, I fell upon a plan of associating him directly with his troops in a bas relief, and thereby reducing his importance. I made a sketch showing this scheme . . . and the monument as it now stands is virtually what I indicated."[26]

In March 1883, while working out his ideas for the monument, Saint-Gaudens wrote that "I have become deeply interested in Colonel Shaw and have worked at the model with an enthusiasm I have not experienced for years."[27] One part of the monument design that was decided upon almost from the beginning was a wide curving arch. In a letter from his wife, Augusta, some months later, she tells him of a grandfather clock she had just purchased (now exhibited at Saint-Gaudens National Historic Site): "The top is shaped precisely as you propose making the top of the Shaw bas relief."[28]

In her doctoral dissertation on Saint-Gaudens, Louis Goldreich Marcus, discusses in depth, the origin of the sculptor's design for the monument. She discovered that the concept of portraying Shaw on horseback with marching soldiers in the background, was probably inspired from a painting Saint-Gaudens saw in the Louvre, *Campagne de France 1814*, by Jean-Louis Ernest Meissonier.[29] This painting depicts Napoleon and his officers on horseback, with rows of infantry in the background. In a letter to his wife's niece, Eugenie Nichols, then in Paris, Saint-Gaudens asked her to secure a photograph of the work for him, and included a quick sketch of the painting in the letter. Although Shaw was on foot during the attack on Fort Wagner, it was normal procedure in most armies for infantry officers to be mounted on horseback while the men were on foot, as was the case when the regiment marched out of Boston in 1863. By portraying Shaw in an equestrian pose Saint-Gaudens was being historically accurate.

Architectural sketch by Henry H. Richardson, 1883. Courtesy Houghton Library, Harvard University, Cambridge, Mass.

Work on the Shaw Memorial, was done entirely at Saint-Gaudens' New York studio at 148 West Thirty Sixth Street. This building was a long, narrow structure that had once served as a painter's supply shed. The Shaw was set against a panel that stretched from wall to wall, about two thirds of the way down the room, and was raised up about four feet from the floor. This arrangement enabled Saint-Gaudens to view the sculpture from a distance at the approximate height it would eventually be installed in Boston.

During the first few years Saint-Gaudens worked on the monument it changed considerably in concept. "In justice to myself I must say here that from the low-relief I proposed making when I undertook the Shaw commission, a relief that reasonably could be finished for the limited sum at the command of the committee, I, through my extreme interest in it and its opportunity, increased the conception until the rider grew almost to a statue in the round and the Negroes assumed far more importance than I had originally intended. Hence the monument, developing in this way infinitely beyond what could be

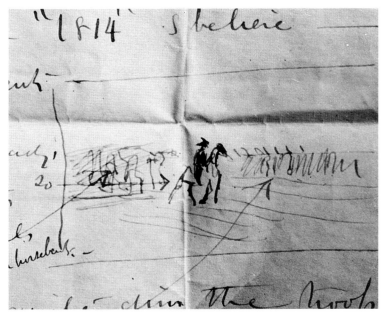

Detail of a letter from Augustus Saint-Gaudens to Eugenie Nichols, with a sketch of the Meissonier painting. Courtesy Special Collections, Dartmouth College Library, Hanover, NH.

Jean-Louis Ernest Meissonier, Campagne de France, 1814. Musée d'Orsay, Paris.

Early pencil sketch (1882) for the Shaw Memorial incorporating ideas from the Meissonier painting. Historic photograph, Saint-Gaudens NHS.

paid for, became a labor of love, and lessened my hesitation in setting it aside at times to make way for more lucrative commissions, commissions that would reimburse me for the pleasure and time I was devoting to this."[30]

The earliest full scale model of the sculpture, though essentially the same composition as the final piece, is in a much lower relief than it eventually evolved. Several other elements that were also later modified are readily noticeable. The angel faces outward, as does one soldier in the second row. The latter gives an almost humorous touch to the work, which was perhaps why it was not retained. The height of the drummers would also be altered to that of boys rather than grown men. In this first version the angel holds flowers, to which a palm frond signifying glory, was later added, and then at the last minute, in early 1897, changed again to an olive branch, for peace.

In working on the relief, as well as with most of his sculpture, Saint-Gaudens was a perfectionist regarding realism, especially with figures. He intentionally wanted to portray a wide range of individuals, both in facial features and age, as were the men of the Fifty-Fourth. This was the first monument depicting blacks where they were not portrayed in a stereotypical manner. Saint-Gaudens hired African American men to pose for him, and subsequently modeled about forty different heads in one third life size, for studies to use while working on the relief. Sixteen of these likenesses appear in the final monument. In all, twenty-one recognizable faces are portrayed among the infantrymen, along with two partial heads in very low relief. Saint-Gaudens remembered that several of the studies which he thought quite good, were not used simply because they did not fit well in the composition.

These models were not professionals, but individuals Saint-Gaudens saw on the street

First full-size model of the Shaw Memorial, mid 1880s.
Courtesy Special Collections, Dartmouth College Library, Hanover, NH.

Early sketch of the angel for the Shaw Memorial. Collection of Saint-Gaudens NHS #1240.

Two rows of soldiers hidden behind the horse and rider and never seen by the viewer of the monument.

who appeared to have just the look he needed for the soldiers. So particular was Saint-Gaudens on this issue, that in 1893 he wrote to his brother-in-law, Thomas J. Homer, in Boston, to ask for his assistance in hiring two men, John Lee and Riley Lee, who worked in Young's Cafe, a Boston restaurant. He had seen them once while dining there and thought them perfect models for the monument.[31]

In his *Reminiscences*, Saint-Gaudens describes his often ineffectual efforts to hire black models. Many of the men suspected the sculptor was up to no good. When several prospective models entered his studio and spied brown painted, plaster heads lying around, they became alarmed and made a quick exit. Finally, someone explained to the bewildered artist, that no doubt these men feared he was a doctor who planned to use their bodies for dissection, a common rumor of the day.

Saint-Gaudens then promised to pay one black man twenty five cents for each model he would bring him. This proved so successful, the next day a large group of African American men congregated in his studio and he was able to choose several that met his needs. Even so, it took several years to complete the studies.

One of the forty study heads created for the Shaw Memorial. Collection of Saint-Gaudens NHS #1439.

Saint-Gaudens' concern for accuracy and realism also extended to the clothing and accessories. Twenty years after the war he still had easy access to examples of the uniforms and equipment needed. With the saddle he was careful to use one of a simple soldier which Shaw used, a type favored by lower ranked officers and unlike what he later used in the Logan and Sherman monuments.[32] At one point he even had someone sketch the original flag of the Fifty-Fourth Regiment at the State House in Boston.

Some of the equipment caused him trouble as he developed the composition, especially the canteens, which he felt produced a "spotty" effect. One day, Frederick MacMonnies, then a sculptural assistant to Saint-Gaudens, was modeling the canteens when Saint-Gaudens complained that he hated the way they looked on the relief. MacMonnies suggested partially covering some of them under the uniforms. This was tried with such satisfaction by Saint-Gaudens, that the idea was quickly adopted. From this episode he went on to develop a system which he termed "fluing," whereby rounding off mechanically straight lines, the uninteresting became slightly hidden and suggestive. He used various ways to break up such lines and also fill in black holes in folds of drapery, which also might detract from the overall effect of the sculpture.[33]

There were other parts of the relief that troubled the artist, some seemingly unimportant. Saint-Gaudens once confided to his later assistant, James Earle Fraser, that there was one particular spot in the group that he felt sure he had worked on more and longer than on all the rest of the monument, it was one of the soldier's pant legs—"it simply would

Clay model of Col. Shaw and his horse, late 1880s.
This part of the monument was completed first. Historic photograph, Saint Gaudens NHS.

not suit him and he was dragged by the impulse toward that particular fold from any other part of the monument that he might be working on. "You know," he told Fraser, " how you callous your hands from using the same tool for a long time. Well, I have a callous on my brain when it comes to that pant leg."[34]

The folds in Shaw's right sleeve and coat were another problem area for the sculptor. He could never seem to get the coat to fall quite the same way during any successive modeling session. Finally, one day, in exasperation, he had one of his assistants, Lyndon Smith, pose for him in the saddle. Smith sat there from 9:00 in the morning straight through until 4:00 P.M. without a movement on his right side, before the modeling of Shaw's clothing was finally done to satisfaction.[35]

When he first began working on the *Shaw Memorial* Saint-Gaudens used the water-based clay commonly employed by sculptors. This had a drawback in that it had to be kept damp at all times, usually by covering the sculpture with wet rags, otherwise the clay would dry and crack. Keeping a work of this size moist was a bothersome and time consuming process. Evidence of cracks are readily visible in the photograph of the first full scale model of the relief. It was probably at about the time this photo was taken that Saint-Gaudens realized that the project would take much longer than he first anticipated, and began to look for an alternative to water-based clay.

The answer to the problem, he knew, was plastoline, an oil-based clay which did not have to be kept moist. It was only produced in France, and for a project this size was prohibitively expensive to import. Instead, Saint-Gaudens and a sculptural assistant, Philip Martiny, developed their own formula for plastoline. This material, still used today by many sculptors, did not dry out with exposure to air and allowed Saint-Gaudens to have the model of the *Shaw Memorial* stand uncovered in his studio for as long as he needed. Once the oil-based clay was perfected, Saint-Gaudens removed the first clay relief and later reconstructed it in plastoline.

After removing the first full scale model, but before it was redone in plastoline, Saint-Gaudens used the same platform to work on the equestrian part of the monument. The horse used for a model was posed on another special platform built about four feet off the ground, the proposed height of the monument. Sometimes when the horse was posed, it was not just hitched by the bridle, but tied in several places to keep it in place. Whenever this was done, the horse protested by constantly stamping its feet and making a continual racket. The horse with the figure of Shaw was the first section finished in final form, after which it was immediately cast in plaster. Later this plaster cast of horse and rider, essentially a sculpture in the round, could be placed in front of the emerging relief to see the effect, and then removed as work progressed on the soldiers and background.

The horse Saint-Gaudens first used as a model was one of his own. ". . . a gray animal which I bought especially for this relief. I used to keep him in an adjoining stable and, at the end of the day, ride him in the park for exercise, thereby accomplishing a double purpose. He died ultimately of pneumonia contracted from a cast I made of him, and I finished my work with a beautiful sorrel I hired at the New York Riding Club."[36] Often, to save time and effort, Saint-Gaudens and other sculptors would take a plaster cast of something they were using in a sculpture, such as articles of clothing, equipment, or even parts of animals and the human body.

Although the monument was to have been completed in two years, the artist ignored the committee and proceeded at his own pace. As the years progressed, the committee became increasingly impatient. In January 1891, Saint-Gaudens wrote to Atkinson that he was working hard on the Shaw and barring illness would have the modeling done in nine months with the casting in bronze an additional three months.[37] By February 1893, he was again writing Atkinson, to assure him that his work on another commission, the World's Columbian Exposition medal, was only done at night, "time taken from my family and social life," and that this in no way interfered with his completion of the Shaw.[38]

Even though work on the relief was proceeding slowly, plans for the architectural setting progressed much more quickly. The setting and surround for the Memorial was designed by Charles Follen Mckim, whose plans were approved by the Boston Art Commission on February 4, 1892. The terrace, granite base, and Tennessee marble surround were then constructed by the Norcross Brothers Contractors of Boston and Worcester. This was all completed by August 25, 1893, at a cost of $19,920 to the city of Boston.[39]

Saint-Gaudens now said that the monument would not be completed by the fall of 1893, but he could promise it by the following May. By October 1893, however, with the relief still not done, several members were proposing that the commission be given to Daniel Chester French, so that "the statue might be ready in the probable lifetime of some members of the committee."[40] Another letter from Atkinson to Charles McKim in 1894, stated in no uncertain terms, ". . . that bronze is wanted pretty damned quick! People are *grumbling* for it, the city *howling* for it, and most of the committee have become *toothless* waiting for it!"[41] This, and other similar comments, spurred Saint-Gaudens to increase his efforts on the monument, but it would still be three more years until the unveiling.

In answer to the criticism of his taking so long on the Shaw Memorial Saint-Gaudens wrote:

> "My own delay I excuse on the ground that a sculptor's work endures for so long that it is next to a crime for him to neglect to do everything that lies in his power to execute a result that will not be a disgrace. There is something extraordinarily irritating, when it is not ludicrous, in a bad statue. It is plastered up before the world to stick and stick for centuries, while man and nations pass away. A poor picture goes into the garret, books are forgotten, but the bronze remains to accuse or shame the populace and perpetuate one of our various idiocies. It is an impertinence and an offense, and that it does not create riots proves the wonderful patience of the human animal."[42]

About this time there were discussions among the committee, the sculptor, and the Shaw family, about the inscriptions to be placed on the front and back of the monument. In June 1894, the committee approved some wording, suggested by Harvard President Charles W. Eliot: "The White Officers: The Black Rank and File: Together." Homer Saint-Gaudens relates that his father's reaction to the wording was that originally the inscriptions for the back of the monument were to be arranged in a manner "most distasteful to him, so he began devious tactics to elude the necessity of placing them in permanent form."[43] Even at the end of February 1897, Saint-Gaudens replied to Atkinson that to put prose lines from Governor Andrew's address on the back above the names of the officers "would be too much inscription on the stone" and "is out of the question to arrange it in this manner."[44]

On the bronze, in the field, Shaw's father suggested the motto of the Society of the Cincinnati, an organization formed after the Revolutionary War for Officers and their descendants, and of whom Robert Gould Shaw was a hereditary member. The inscription, OMNIA RELINQVIT SERVARE REMPVBLICAM (He forsook all to preserve the public weal), was indeed used, though the Latin is grammatically incorrect. In December 1898, the City of Boston Art Commission wrote to Saint-Gaudens in Paris, to say that they had been informed by scholars that the Latin was not proper. Perhaps feeling somewhat embarrassed, the committee wanted to correct the inscription. Their suggestion was for the artist to model the letters "adpetens" and insert it after relinquit, (eagerly desiring). This, they felt, would be the easiest and most cost effective way to make the change.[45] The suggestion was never carried out. Although incorrect, the Latin phrase is the motto of the Society of the Cincinnati, and no doubt Saint-Gaudens felt more comfortable leaving it unchanged. Among the other symbolic details on the relief, are the thirty four stars along the upper edge representing the states of the Union in 1863.

It was the angel that caused Saint-Gaudens the most problems in the relief's composition. His sister-in-law, Elisabeth Nichols, wrote from Cornish in August, 1895, "he has been working on the allegorical figure of the 'Shaw' and apparently finds it difficult to make it suit his idea. He was getting rather discouraged so he is coming here to stay until the middle of September hoping I suppose to go back refreshed."[46] For the face of the angel, he first used the head of Annie Page, one of his models. He soon admitted that this became too much like a portrait for him, so in the end relied on his imagination for the features. Several of his friends later suggested that the angel somewhat resembled his mother and also a former model in Paris. At the end of December, Saint-Gaudens wrote to Atkinson that the "floating figure" is almost done and "I'm joyous about it. I have got it at last. 'I have got it solid' as they say. I at last have what I want in it. It's a matter of cleaning it up and pulling it together now and very shortly I shall write to you 'finis'."[47]

On May 8, 1896, Saint-Gaudens is finally able to report that the Shaw has been done for some time but a constructional difficulty will delay its being molded for a few more weeks. He assured Atkinson it had nothing to do with the artistic portion, "that is complete." He added that the delay was inconveniencing him financially, and requested the sum due on finishing of the clay—he would be happy with $500 or $1,000.[48]

Soon after reporting the Shaw complete, Saint Gaudens decided to slightly alter the size of the ever troubling angel. This prompted an angry response from Atkinson on June 5, "We are all appalled and disheartened . . . by learning . . . that you have again decided to reconstruct that angel. . . . Members of the committee are hopeless of your ever being able to complete this work."[49] The next day in another letter he told the artist "You and I are now at the parting of the ways," and added that "one person in a hundred thousand would ever know the difference in the angel's size."[50] Two days later, Saint-Gaudens responded with a telegram that he would agree to go ahead with the monument the way it was with no more changes to the angel.[51]

On October 10, Saint-Gaudens was visited by William A. Coffin, who was preparing an article on the sculptor and the Shaw Memorial. Coffin remarked in the article, that the finishing touches were put on the monument that very day, which by coincidence was Shaw's birthday. The angel as completed at this time, faced outward as in the early sketches. In her left arm she holds a palm frond, signifying victory or glory, as well as poppies denoting death. The lower half of the body and its drapery is positioned well above the level of the rifles and figures. This first completed version of the Shaw Memorial is known only from photographs taken in preparation for Coffin's extensive article in the June, 1897, issue of *Century Magazine*.[52]

Just as the monument appeared to be finally complete, and Saint-Gaudens satisfied with his work, he received a letter from the French sculptor, Paul Bion. A long time friend, Bion's artistic criticism was particularly valued by Saint-Gaudens. After seeing photographs of the earliest version of the Shaw, Bion wrote that "I had no need of your 'nom de Dieu' allegory on the ceiling. Your Negroes marching in step and your Colonel leading them told me enough. Your priestess merely bores me as she tries to impress upon me the beauty of their action."[53]

Though he had assured the committee that the sculpture was finished, Saint-Gaudens was at heart still ambivalent about the angel. Bion's comments had a profound impression on him, and he once again turned his attentions to the floating figure, making significant changes. The palm frond was replaced by an olive branch, signifying peace, the angel's face was directed forward, adding to the motion of the piece, and the drapery of the angel's robes was modified.[54] He even took the opportunity to simplify the folds in the back of Shaw's coat where it covered the saddle. In a letter to his niece, Rose Nichols, he wrote of Bion's comments, that "I am not disturbed by his dislike of my figure. It is because it does not look well in the photograph. If the figure in itself looked well, he would have liked it I know. . . . I still think that a figure, if well done in that relation to the rest of the scheme, is a fine thing to do. The Greeks and Romans did it finely in their sculpture. After all it's the way the thing's done that makes it right or wrong, that's about the only creed I have in art."[55]

Unknown to Saint-Gaudens, Bion was dead by the time he had received his letter. Later, on February 17, 1897, he wrote to Rose Nichols, "Today, however, I have had a kind of sad feeling of companionship with him that seems to bring him to me, in working over the head of the flying figure of the 'Shaw.' The bronze founders are not ready for it yet. I have had a stamp made of the figure, and I am sure you will think I have helped it a great deal. You know that Thayer [Abbot Thayer] told me he thought an idea I once had of turning the head more in profile, was a better one than that I had evolved, and I've always wished to do it. It is done, and it's the feeling of death and mystery and love, in the making of it, that brought my friend back to me so much to-day."[56]

Saint-Gaudens worked steadily on the relief, "I shall be all the week at the figure. I've made an olive-branch instead of the palm,—it looks less "Christian martyr-like" and I have lightened and simplified the drapery a great deal. I had not seen it for two or three months and I had a fresh impression."[57] Homer notes that his father worked on the figure to such an extent "he became mentally blind to the result and to the aspect of the composition." Even when the workmen came to pick up the cast for shipment to the foundry, in December 1897, Saint-Gaudens made them wait while he made last minute changes.

During the winter, while other parts of the relief were being cast, he continued to work on the angel, and by late February was able to send the modified figure to the foundry for casting in place of the original version. As he felt rushed to complete the monument, Saint-Gaudens was never fully satisfied with the angel, nor of the way the monument appeared in Boston, and it would continue to haunt him for the remainder of his life.

James Earle Fraser recalled that Saint-Gaudens was especially delighted with criticisms of the Shaw provided by two of his other friends. He once asked Kenyon Cox what he thought about the piece, to which Cox replied that it was good, and was going along alright, and was sure it would come out well in the end. Saint-Gaudens was a little irritated and said " You are not very enthusiastic about it, are you Cox?" to which Cox replied "I am not really enthusiastic by nature—I am quiet and reserved." Just then Saint-Gaudens' dog, Doodles, came into the studio and Cox immediately began joyfully playing with the dog exclaiming " what a grand and wonderful dog!" Saint-Gaudens said "Oh, no, Cox you are not enthusiastic, you are very reserved."[59]

George DeForest Brush, however, appeared somewhat upset by the monument. Saint-Gaudens questioned him about this, to which Brush replied "Do you really want to know?" Saint-Gaudens said "Certainly, I want to know." "Well, then" said Brush, "Take out the horse!"[60]

Joy at the completion of the monument was deeply felt. McKim wrote Saint-Gaudens on September 3, 1896, "Heaven be praised . . . ! I can hardly believe my eyes and am overjoyed to hear that the Shaw is really done—on your account and that of the surviving members of the committee . . ."[61]

The bronze cast was completed in May 1897, by the Gorham Manufacturing Company at their foundry in Providence, Rhode Island, at a cost of $7,000. This may have been a reduced fee, as the committee was hoping that the company would produce the complicated cast " for glory not profit." Atkinson wrote to them that he knew "it will be a difficult casting and very likely you may not make anything on it . . . yet it is a great work and well worth doing."[62]

The cast was brought to Boston and installed on Friday, May 21, just a week before the unveiling. The patination was only applied that weekend, once the bronze was in place. Saint-Gaudens came to Boston with his assistant, Gaeton Ardisson, to oversee the process. Quick repairs were also necessary to the stonework which was completed in 1893, but had stood empty and exposed to the weather for three years. During this time the monument was screened from prying eyes by a large cloth strung between the two large English elm trees that framed the site, and are still there today.

Veterans of the Fifty-Fourth Massachusetts Regiment march past the Shaw Memorial at the unveiling. May 31, 1897.
Boston Sunday Journal, June 6, 1897.

THE UNVEILING

Many of them were bent and crippled, many with white heads, some with bouquets ... The impression of those old soldiers, passing the very spot where they left for the war so many years before, thrills me even as I write these words. They faced and saluted the relief, with the music playing "John Brown's Body," a recall of what I had heard and seen thirty years before from my cameo-cutter's window. They seemed as if returning from the war, the troops of bronze marching in the opposite direction, the direction in which they had left for the front, and the young men there represented now showing these veterans the vigor and hope of youth. It was a consecration.[65]

—Augustus Saint-Gaudens, May 31, 1897

On May 31, 1897, the day of the unveiling, it was gray and overcast with a light misty rain, though Saint-Gaudens commented that this was better for viewing the monument than bright sunshine. In spite of the weather there was a festive air about the occasion, and many people lined the streets. Fortunately the rain stopped by the beginning of the ceremony. The parade began at 10:00 A.M. as the Governor and various dignitaries took their place in carriages at the corner of Dartmouth and Commonwealth. Present in the reviewing party were Saint-Gaudens, Booker T. Washington, Mayor Quincy, Prof. William James, various military officers, and members of the Memorial Committee.

After the parade passed the reviewing location, the carriages conveying the dignitaries moved to the site of the monument, where the men took their places across the street on the State House steps. Every available space along the street, and on the grounds of the State House was occupied. Onlookers also filled the windows and balconies of the State House, with a few of the more adventurous on the roof.

Veteran officers of the Fifty-Fourth in front of the monument, May 31, 1897. Courtesy Commonwealth of Massachusetts, Massachusetts Art Commission.

The memorial was covered by two large American flags. At exactly 11:17 A.M., a signal was given by committee chairman, Colonel Henry Lee, and the ropes to drop the flags were pulled by two young men stationed at the monument, both nephews of Robert Gould Shaw. As the sculpture was revealed, the crowd cheered, the Germania Band began to play "The Battle Hymn of the Republic" and a battery of artillery on the Common fired a seventeen gun salute. Simultaneously a signalman positioned on the State House roof, waved a white flag to alert other signalmen on the Ames building. There a large flag was dropped, to signal three Naval warships in the harbor, the U.S.S. Massachusetts, the New York and the Texas, which then each fired a twenty one gun salute.[63]

A brief ceremony then took place where Colonel Lee, on behalf of the committee, presented the Memorial to Governor Roger Wolcott, who accepted on behalf of the Commonwealth. Lee spoke, "Friends, more than twenty years ago these subscribers appointed a committee with full powers to procure a fitting testimonial to Colonel Robert Gould Shaw and his brave black soldiers. That committee has completed its task.   Your honor has witnessed the unveiling of the monument and will, I am sure, congratulate us that, thanks to the sculptor, we have builded better than we knew."[64]

The dozen or more military units present then began to march again, now past the

Back of the Shaw Memorial showing the inscriptions. Architectural design by Charles F. McKim.
The American Architect and Building News, September 11, 1897.

Memorial. Included were contingents of cadets, naval seaman from the warships, and 900 members of the New York Seventh Regiment, the regiment Shaw first joined during the war. Sixty-five veterans of the Massachusetts Fifty-Fourth Regiment led the parade. Some of their officers wore their Civil War uniforms, but most of the enlisted men were in their best frock coats. Black veterans from the Fifty-Fifth Massachusetts and the Fifth Cavalry were also present. Among the men of the Fifty-Fourth was Sergeant Carney carrying the American Flag. The sight of him and the flag elicited cheers from many of the onlookers who knew of his exploits.

After the parade, the veterans of the Fifty-Fourth laid a large wreath of Lilies of the Valley before the monument. Saint-Gaudens was deeply moved by the sight of the men.

After the parade, and a special lunch for the veterans of the three African American Regiments, the festivities continued in the Music Hall. The building was packed with an enthusiastic audience as the ceremonies began at 12:30 P.M. and the chorus sang "Our Heroes" and "Battle Hymn of the Republic." Saint-Gaudens was extremely uncomfortable with such occasions, and he purposely arrived late so as to avoid having to sit on the podium. He was recognized, however, and quickly brought to the forefront with even more notice than if he had arrived early. When introduced by the Governor, Saint-

Portrait relief of Charles F. McKim
by Augustus Saint-Gaudens., 1878.
Collection Saint-Gaudens NHS #72.

Gaudens received a thunderous, standing ovation. He remembered that "it was an awful moment, but it would be stupid to deny that at the same time it was thrilling to hear the great storm of applause and cheering that I faced."[66] He also made sure to comment to the press that the architect Charles F. McKim also deserved a great deal of credit and his contributions should not be forgotten.

Other speakers that afternoon included Prof. William James, whose brother, Garth Wilkinson James, an officer with the Fifty-Fourth, had been severely wounded at Fort Wagner. He said of the monument, "And this, fellow-citizens, is why after the great generals have had their monuments, and long after the abstract common soldiers' monuments have been reared on every village green, we have chosen to take Shaw and Shaw's regiment as the subjects of the first soldier's monument to be raised to a particular set of comparatively undistinguished men."[67]

The other featured speaker was Booker T. Washington, president of Tuskegee Institute, and one of the most celebrated African Americans of his day. He too gave a stirring and eloquent oration that was very well received. Also on the podium to receive the acclamation of the crowd was Sergeant Carney.

Soon after the dedication, Colonel Henry Lee edited the complete proceedings of the ceremony, which was then published in a finely bound, hundred page book, *The Monument to Robert Gould Shaw*, by the Houghton Mifflin Riverside Press in Boston. Included are the full texts of speeches, the inscriptions on the monument, and the official guest list.

Accolades on the memorial came from all over. Henry James, then in Europe, saw a reproduction of the Shaw in *Harper's Weekly*, "How I rejoice that something really fine is to stand there forever for R.G.S. and all the rest of them. This thing of Saint-Gaudens strikes me as real perfection." [68] Artist and critic, Kenyon Cox, commented that "people say it's the best thing that Saint-Gaudens ever did. For my part no one anywhere in any country has ever done any better."[69]

Shaw's widow, Anne, now an invalid and living in Cannes, France, did not attend the unveiling. She was sent photos of the monument, but her reaction was never recorded.[70] Shaw's parents were still living, and shortly after the unveiling, Shaw's mother asked Saint-Gaudens to visit her. She explained that although only a bas-relief had been planned, she knew that he had spent much time and money on the project, and she wished to add her personal check to the amount he had been paid.[3] In his speech during the unveiling ceremony, Colonel Henry Lee quoted her as saying to the sculptor,

"You have immortalized my native city; you have immortalized my dear son; you have immortalized yourself."[71]

The editor, Richard Watson Gilder, composed a poem about the monument, "Robert Gould Shaw" which affected Saint-Gaudens deeply. He wrote to Gilder "that anything I have done should have suggested the inspired and inspiring ode . . . makes all the great strain and love gone to the making of the 'Shaw' worthwhile, and I have not lived entirely in vain."[72]

PARIS

Following the unveiling of the *Shaw Memorial* in May, and the dedication in July of his monument to General John Logan, in Chicago's Grant Park, Saint-Gaudens began preparing for his move to Paris in October. He had tired of New York, and felt he needed to return to Europe. While his work was praised in America, he felt that he needed to measure himself and his art against his contemporaries in Europe where he was less well known.

Between 1896 and 1897, he prepared a complete plaster cast of the Shaw, no doubt with the intention of bringing it to France. In December 1897, he arranged for shipment of this cast from his New York studio along with other plaster casts, including among other pieces, the *Puritan, Amor Caritas* and the *Sherman Monument.*[73]

Sculpture court in the Grand Palais, Exposition Universelle, Paris, 1900.
The Shaw Memorial is to the left at the top of the stairway.

The Shaw Memorial at the Exposition Universelle, 1900.
(Report of the Commissioner-General for the
United States to the International Universal Exposition, Paris, 1900, Volume I)

The Shaw arrived in Paris by February 1898, and was assembled in the studio Saint-Gaudens established in the Rue de Bagneux. Here he worked on some of the changes he had been thinking about since the unveiling in Boston. In April, a reworked *Shaw Memorial* was exhibited at the Paris Salon. In this third version, two noticeable changes had been made in the sculptor's unending quest for perfection. First, the angel was lowered slightly in the background, and the drapery simplified. Second, the horse's mane which had lain down across the neck, was now made to flow towards the rear to further emphasize the forward motion.

For the next two years the cast remained in his Paris studio where he continued to work on it, along with other sculptures including the *Amor Caritas* and the *Sherman Monument*. In April, 1900, he once again exhibited the *Shaw Memorial* in Paris, at the great *Exposition Universelle*, one of the largest expositions of its time. It was only then, after seventeen years, that Saint-Gaudens finally considered the *Shaw Memorial* finished.

The relief was located at the top of a staircase in the Grand Palais, just outside the doorway to the United States exhibits area. Positioned to the other side of this doorway was the *Amor Carita*s or "Angel With Tablet," which the French Government later purchased for the Luxembourg Museum collection. The great central area below on the ground floor, was filled with sculpture, including a full sized plaster cast of the *Sherman Monument*. The Sherman would be unveiled three years later in New York's Grand Army Plaza.

Saint-Gaudens had four major works in the 1900 exposition: the *Shaw Memorial*, the *Sherman Monument*, the *Puritan* and the *Amor Caritas*. He received the Grand Prix and a gold medal for his works, and was awarded the Legion of Honor (officier), a coveted award infrequently given to foreigners. It was in Paris that the sculptor Auguste Rodin, saw the *Shaw Memorial* and doffed his hat in tribute to it as a great masterpiece.

The *Shaw Memorial* was now in its fourth and final form. Since its exhibition two years before, Saint-Gaudens had again changed the angel slightly; straightening the right knee somewhat, and lowering the whole figure so that the drapery now extended down to top of the rifles. He also moved the two flags closer together and changed the position of the sword so that the blade was parallel to the relief. Along the base was added the lettering "ROBERT GOULD SHAW KILLED WHILE LEADING THE ASSAULT ON FORT WAGNER JULY TWENTY THIRD EIGHTEEN HUNDRED SIXTY THREE AUGUSTUS SAINT-GAUDENS MDCCCLXXXXVII." (Although the inscription on the Boston monument gives the correct date of the battle, July 18, 1863, for some reason it was changed to July 23, in this wording and never corrected).[74]

Even after initial installation at the Paris Exposition, Saint-Gaudens was not satisfied with the color of the Shaw. The painter, William A. Coffin, wrote of seeing him just before the exposition opened: "He stood at the top of the great staircase leading from the sculpture court in the Grand Palais, directing two men who were coloring the big cast of the Shaw which stood there at the entrance to the galleries occupied by the United States section in paintings. The Shaw had been colored. It was all set up and it was all 'finished.' But Saint-Gaudens told me he thought it was too dark and he was having it all gone over with tint and rub-down to make it lighter. As usual he was pursuing perfection."[75]

Saint-Gaudens was particularly concerned with the patination and resulting color of the surface. Throughout his life he used a number of different colors of patina on both the bronze and plaster casts used for exhibition. He especially disliked leaving plaster casts white, because of the condition after being exhibited when they became dusty. He modified the color of the Shaw plaster cast several times (1898, 1900, 1905). Once, when asked about producing additional plaster casts of the Shaw, he wrote "I have a horror of the exhibition of my work in plaster, particularly, if it is to be permanent and unless the Shaw is colored, as is the replica at Buffalo, I could not consent to its reproduction."[76]

BUFFALO

William Alexander Coffin, a painter, writer and art critic, had been appointed Fine Arts Director of the Pan American Exposition planned for Buffalo, New York in 1901. While in Paris visiting the *Exposition Universelle*, he persuaded Saint-Gaudens to exhibit some of his best work at the Exposition in Buffalo, in particular, casts of those pieces shown in Paris. Coffin was particularly familiar with the *Shaw Memorial*, having written an extensive article on the sculpture and Saint-Gaudens for *Century Magazine* in 1897. He considered it a great coup to have acquired the Shaw and Sherman for display at the exposition.

The requested casts, including the *Shaw Memorial*, the *Sherman Monument*, the *Puritan*, and the *Amor Caritas*, arrived in Buffalo by April 1901. The *Shaw Memorial* was placed at the end of the Sculpture Court in the Fine Arts Building. Saint-Gaudens sent one of his young sculptural assistants, Henry Hering, to Buffalo to help assemble the Shaw, make necessary repairs, and match the bronze color along the reconstructed seams.

The Pan American Exposition opened on May 1, 1901, but the hurriedly erected Fine Arts Building was still unfinished. Hanging of the art exhibits was not begun until May 22, two days after Dedication Day. Formal opening ceremonies for the building finally took place on June 15, and the Fine Arts Building opened to the general public two days later. In a snapshot taken at the opening day ceremony, one can see the Shaw cast assembled and in the process of retouching. The relief is roped off, and a workman is standing in front.

At the close of the Exposition, Coffin was persistent in trying to persuade Saint-Gaudens to leave the Sherman and Shaw casts in Buffalo. As the Sherman was not yet complete, Saint-Gaudens insisted upon its return to Cornish. The Shaw, too, he wanted returned, unless he were reimbursed in the amount of $2,000. He explained that there was interest from several museums, including the Art Institute of Chicago and the Dresden Museum, for casts of the Shaw, and it would cost him that much to prepare a new cast and mold from one he had in Cornish. After some negotiations, the cast was purchased by the Albright Knox Art Gallery for the requested $2,000. Other casts of the Shaw, however, were never made, although he had contacted Gaeton Ardisson, his long-time plaster casting assistant, still attending to Saint-Gauden's affairs in Paris, to come to Cornish with the intention of making casts.[77]

Until 1902, Saint-Gaudens exhibited the original plaster cast of the second version of the Shaw in the "Large Studio" in Cornish. In a letter to William Coffin in December, 1901, he refers to it as a cast of the "imperfect original."[78] Sometime before 1905 he had it destroyed and buried nearby.[79] The original mold of the second version was returned from the foundry, but this too he destroyed soon after his return from Paris. No doubt he wanted to ensure that no other cast of the second version of the Shaw, which he considered flawed, could be easily produced.

The Shaw cast in Buffalo was moved to the new Albright Art Gallery building in mid December 1901, where it was set up. The Albright building had originally been intended to serve as the Fine Arts building for the Pan American Exposition, but because

Formal opening day of the Fine Arts Building, Pan American Exposition, Buffalo, NY, June 15, 1901.
Final touches are still being made on the Monument. The building was opened to the public two days later.
Courtesy Special Collections, Dartmouth College Library, Hanover, NH.

The Sculpture Court, Fine Arts Building, Pan American Exposition, Buffalo, New York. June 1901.
(Frontispiece, Catalog of the Exhibition of Fine Arts, Pan American Exposition, 1901)

Bronze cast of the angel from the fourth and final version of the Shaw Memorial, H. 35¹³⁄₁₆", w 9'8¹⁄₁₆".
Made from molds taken in Buffalo 1904/5. Acquired by the Brooklyn Museum from Mrs. Augustus Saint-Gaudens, 1923.
Courtesy Brooklyn Museum, Robert B. Woodward Memorial Fund.

of a shortage of material, the building was not completed until 1905. Prior to the opening of the Albright's inaugural exhibition, the museum decided to relocate the relief to another spot within the building. This last minute decision to move the piece was made in the midst of applying a new surface treatment of gold leaf with a bronze tone glaze. Saint-Gaudens had sent another of his assistants, James Earle Fraser, to "bronze" the piece after the gilding, and thus achieve the preferred effect.[80] The artist himself, stricken with cancer, was now too ill to make the trip.

In 1904, Saint-Gaudens engaged the firm of Casteras Brothers of New York City, to send a man to Buffalo to make a plaster piece mold and cast of the angel. This first mold was not entirely satisfactory, so in 1905, he asked the Albright Museum that another mold be made and Joseph Balk of Buffalo, was hired to do the work.[81]

James Earle Fraser recalled that Saint-Gaudens never finished the Shaw to his satisfaction, and that while in Paris he remodeled the angel with the intention of cutting it out of the bronze in Boston and replacing it with the final version. This was no doubt the reason he later had molds made of the angel in 1904/5. A bronze cast made from this mold at a later date, was sold in 1923 by his widow, Augusta Homer Saint-Gaudens to the Brooklyn Museum.

The Shaw Memorial was exhibited at the Albright Knox Art Gallery from 1905 until 1919, when a wall was erected in front of the monument so that the gallery could be used for other exhibitions. The relief remained hidden for thirty years. In 1945, the Trustees of the Saint-Gaudens Memorial began negotiations to acquire the *Shaw Memorial* cast for the Saint-Gaudens Memorial in Cornish, New Hampshire. The previous year, the "Studio of the Caryatids" at Cornish had burned to the ground, with the loss of many large plaster casts. The Memorial was planning to build a new exhibition gallery and was anxious to include casts of some of Saint-Gaudens' well known public monuments. It was not until January 1949, however, that the Shaw was finally dismantled and shipped to Cornish. The work was directed by Joseph Balk, now age seventy-three, who had dismantled and relocated the relief to the Albright Gallery in 1901.

Shaw Memorial on display at the Inaugural Exhibition, Albright Knox Art Gallery, Buffalo, NY, 1905.

The Shaw Memorial, fourth version, as it was exhibited at Cornish, NH, 1959-1996.

CORNISH

The cast arrived in Cornish in late January 1949, but because of financial con-
straints, remained in storage until the summer of 1959. Following a fund raising
campaign and design of an open protective pavilion by the New York firm of Platt
Brothers Architects, sculptor John Terken of New York, was hired to install the relief at
the end of the "Bowling Green," a long, rectangular garden area enclosed by twelve foot
high hedges. With a hired assistant, Terken worked for fourteen days to piece the monument back together. Extensive restoration was needed along the joints and damaged
areas of the base and background. Because of the expense of replicating the gold leaf,
the sculpture was painted a green color to simulate oxidized bronze. Terken returned in
1962, to make repairs and touch up the surface, damaged somewhat by exposure to the
elements.

In 1965, the Trustees of the Saint-Gaudens Memorial donated the site and its collections, to the National Park Service, and it became the Saint-Gaudens National Historic
Site. Other than occasional minor repairs to the surface, no action was taken with the
cast until 1981. That year, the National Park Service engaged the Center of Conservation

cast until 1981. That year, the National Park Service engaged the Center of Conservation and Technical Services, Fogg Art Museum at Harvard University, to restore the surface patination of gilded bronze.

By 1993, it was clear that the plaster cast could not remain outdoors for much longer without suffering extensive damage because of uncontrolled environmental conditions. The Saint-Gaudens Memorial Trustees, in collaboration with the National Park Service, began a campaign to raise funds to replicate the plaster in bronze. The plaster would be conserved and placed on long term loan to the National Gallery of Art. The Modern Art Foundry of Long Island City, New York was contracted to cast the bronze from molds made by the Robert Shure, Skylight Studios of Woburn, Massachusetts.

It was fitting that on the one hundredth anniversary of the *Shaw Memorial's* dedication in Boston, a new bronze cast of the artist's final creative efforts on this masterpiece was unveiled at the Saint-Gaudens National Historic Site in Cornish, New Hampshire. These events surrounding the *Shaw Memorial* demonstrate a new appreciation and recognition of both the sculpture and what it signifies. The plaster and the bronze casts of the final, and to the sculptor's mind, perfected, version of this great monument will now be seen and enjoyed by generations to come.

Gregory C. Schwarz
Chief of Interpretation
Saint-Gaudens NHS

ENDNOTES

1. Burchard, Peter, *One Gallant Rush: Robert Gould Shaw and His Brave Black Regiment*, New York; St. Martin's Press, 1965, p. 57

2. Craig, Tom, *Colored Volunteer*, Sheet Music, Philadelphia, 1863, Broadsides Collection, John Hay Library, Brown University

3. Burchard, p. 94

4. Emilio, Luis F., *A Brave Black Regiment: History of the Fifty-Fourth Regiment of Massachusetts Volunteer Infantry 1863-1865:* Boston; Boston Book Company, 1894, p. 392

5. Ibid. p. 72

6. Ibid. p. 78

7. Ibid. p. 82

8. Brown, William Wells, *The Negro in the American Rebellion: His Heroism and his Fidelity*, Boston; Lee & Shepard, 1867, p.201

9. Cox, Clinton, *Undying Glory: The Story of the Massachusetts 54th Regiment*, New York; Scholastic, Inc. 1991, p. 96

10. Emilio, p. 95

11. Hine, Darlene Clark, ed. *Black Women in America: An Historical Encyclopedia,* Brooklyn, Carlson Publishing Inc., 1993, p. 1179

12. Emilio, p. 99

13. Emilio, p. 102-103

14. Emilio, p. 392

15. Wade, Hugh Mason, *A Brief History of Cornish, 1763-1974*, Hanover; University Press of New England, 1976, p.38

16. Emilio, p. 94

17. During the war the Fifty-Fourth had a total enrollment o f 1,354. Of these, five officers and ninety-five men were confirmed killed in action, or died of their wounds. Another fifty-seven were listed as missing, of which nineteen were later reported to have died in prison. Thirty others were captured and later exchanged or released at the end of the war. Twenty officers and 274 men were wounded, and another seventy-five succumbed to dis-

In 1996, the Civil War Soldiers and Sailors project created a computerized data bank listing all known names of men in the United States Colored Troops. These names are available for searching through the Internet. Eventually the names of all Union and Confederate soldiers and sailors will be placed into this databank.

18. Kirstein, Lincoln, *Lay This Laurel*: New York; Eakins Press, 1973

19. Emilio, p.102-103

20. *The Monument to Robert Gould Shaw: Its Inception, Completion and Unveiling 1865- 1897*: Boston; Houghton Mifflin and Co., 1897, p.1

21. Ibid, p.8

22. Emerson-Nichols Papers, Schlesinger Library, Radcliffe College, Cambridge, Massachusetts, Letter from Augustus Saint-Gaudens to Edward Atkinson, December 5, 1882.

23. Ibid. Letter from Augustus Saint-Gaudens to Edward Atkinson, October 3, 1883.

24. The Papers of Augustus Saint-Gaudens, Special Collections, Dartmouth College Library, Hanover, New Hampshire. Contract between Saint-Gaudens and the Shaw Memorial Committee.

25. Saint-Gaudens, Homer, ed. *The Reminiscences of Augustus Saint-Gaudens*, New York; The Century Co., 1913, v. 1, p. 332

26. Ibid, v. 1, p. 332

27. Emerson-Nichols papers, Letter from Augustus Saint-Gaudens to Edward Atkinson, March 19, 1883

28. Letter from Augusta Saint-Gaudens to Augustus Saint-Gaudens, September 2, 1883. The Papers of Augustus Saint-Gaudens, Special Collections, Baker Library, Dartmouth College, Hanover, New Hampshire

29. Dartmouth, Letter from Augustus Saint-Gaudens to Eugenie Nichols. See also, Marcus, Lois Goldreich, "The Shaw Memorial by Augustus Saint-Gaudens: A History Painting in Bronze," *Winterthur Portfolio*, v. XIV, No. 1, pp 1-24

30. Saint-Gaudens, v. 1, p. 333

31. Ibid. v. 1, pp. 337-338. There is no record of whether these men ever posed for Saint-Gaudens, and none of the other model's names are known.

32. Dartmouth, Letter from Augustus Saint-Gaudens to Gaeton Ardisson, November 14, 1897

33. Saint-Gaudens, v.1, pp. 343-343

34. Autobiography, manuscript. The Papers of James Earle Fraser, Special Collections, Syracuse University, Syracuse, New York

35. Saint-Gaudens, v. 1, p. 343

36. Ibid, v. 1, p. 333

37. Emerson-Nichols papers, Letter from Augustus Saint-Gaudens to Edward Atkinson, January 20, 1891.

38. Ibid. Letter from Augustus Saint-Gaudens to Edward Atkinson, February 11, 1893

39. Kirstein

40. Wilkinson, p.282

41. Letter from Charles F. McKim to Augustus Saint-Gaudens, Box #1, late 1894, Charles Follen McKim Papers, Library of Congress, Washington, D.C.

42. Saint-Gaudens, v. 2, p. 78-79

43. Ibid, v. 2, p.88

44. Emerson-Nichols papers, Letter Augustus Saint-Gaudens to Edward Atkinson, February 21, 1897

45. Dartmouth, Letter from the City of Boston Art Commission to Augustus Saint-Gaudens, December 9, 1898

46. Emerson-Nichols papers, Letter from Lizzie Nichols to her husband?, August, 1895

47. Ibid., Letter from Augustus Saint-Gaudens to Edward Atkinson, December 31, 1895

48. Ibid, Letter from Augustus Saint-Gaudens to Edward Atkinson, May 8, 1896

49. Ibid, Letter from Edward Atkinson to Augustus Saint-Gaudens, June 5, 1896

50. Wilkinson, p. 284

51. Ibid, p. 284

52. Coffin, William A., "The Shaw Memorial And the Sculptor St. Gaudens," *Century Illustrated Magazine*, v. XXXII, June, 1897 p. 176-177, 179-186, 194-200. Once the changes were made other photographs of the relief were made after the unveiling. A doctored photograph also appeared in a Harpers Weekly issue just prior to the unveiling. In this, the 1896 photo was used but the angel cut out and replaced with the final version used in the bronze. This was all done without Saint-Gaudens consent and he was quite angered over the affair.

53. Saint-Gaudens, v. 1, p. 344

54. Though Homer Saint-Gaudens refers to this as a laurel branch, Augustus himself, calls it an olive branch.

55. Saint-Gaudens, v. 1, p. 344

56. Nichols, Rose Standish, "Familiar Letters of Augustus Saint-Gaudens," McClure's Magazine, v. XXXI, October, 1908, No. 6,   pp. 603-616, Letter from Augustus Saint-Gaudens to Rose Nichols, February 17, 1897

57. Saint-Gaudens, v. 1, p. 343

58. Rose Nichols, Letter from Augustus Saint-Gaudens to Rose Nichols, February 17, 1897

59. James Earle Fraser Papers. Autobiography
60. Ibid
61. McKim Papers. Letter from Charles F. McKim to Augustus Saint-Gaudens, September 3, 1896
62. Wilkinson, p. 285
63. Monument, p. 47
64. Ibid. p. 60
65. Saint-Gaudens, v. 2, p. 83
66. Ibid, v. 2, p. 84
67. Monument, p. 84
68. Kirstein, p.78
69. Saint-Gaudens, v. 2, p. 94
70. Gilchrist, Marianne McLeod, "The Shaw Family of Staten Island: Elizabeth Gaskell's American Friends, *The Gaskell Society Journal*, v. IX, 1995, pp. 1-12. Mrs. Shaw died in Boston in 1907 and is buried in Lenox, Mass.
71. Monument, p. 60
72. Saint-Gaudens, v. 1, p. 347
73. Museum Archives, The Museum of Fine Arts, Boston, Massachusetts. Saint-Gaudens arranged with the Director, Mr. Loring, to have "Chico," the museum's packer go to the sculptor's New York studio in December, 1897, to pack and ship the Shaw cast to Paris.
74. An article in the 1898 Gazette des Beaux Arts also mentioned that the twenty-third was the date of the battle. By 1898, Saint-Gaudens apparently had forgotten the actual date and used this by mistake.
75. Dartmouth, Saint-Gaudens papers, "Reminiscences of Augustus Saint-Gaudens" by William Coffin
76. Ibid. Letter from Augustus Saint-Gaudens to John M. Beatty, Carnegie Institute, March 31, 1904
77. Ibid. Letter from Augustus Saint-Gaudens to William A. Coffin, November 2, 1901
78. Ibid.
79. James Earle Fraser Papers.
80. Dartmouth, Saint-Gaudens Papers, Letter from Edward B. Green to Augustus Saint-Gaudens, July, 1905
81. Ibid, Letter from Augustus Saint-Gaudens to Albright Art Gallery

BIBLIOGRAPHY

Adams, Virginia M. ed. *On the Altar of Freedom: A Black Soldier's Civil War Letters From the Front*; Amherst; University of Massachusetts Press, 1991

Axelrod, Steven, "Colonel Shaw in American Poetry: 'For the Union Dead' and its Precursors," *American Quarterly*, v. XXIV, No. 4, October 1972, pp. 523-537

Burchard, Peter, *One Gallant Rush: Robert Gould Shaw and His Brave Black Regiment*, New York; St. Martin's Press, 1965

Brown, William Wells, *The Negro in the American Rebellion: His Heroism and his Fidelity*, Boston; Lee & Shepard, 1867

Catalogue of the Exhibition of Fine Arts: Pan American Exposition, Buffalo, 1901, Buffalo; 1901

Coffin, William A., "The Shaw Memorial And the Sculptor St. Gaudens," *Century Illustrated Magazine*, v. XXXII, June, 1897 p. 176-177, 179-186, 194-200

Cox, Clinton, *Undying Glory: The Story of the Massachusetts 54th Regiment*, New York; Scholastic, Inc. 1991

Dryfhout, John H. *The Work of Augustus Saint-Gaudens*, Hanover; University Press of New England, 1982

Duncan, Russell, ed. *Blue-Eyed Child of Fortune: The Civil War Letters of Colonel Robert Gould Shaw*, Athens; The University of Georgia Press, 1992

Emilio, Luis F., *A Brave Black Regiment: History of the Fifty-Fourth Regiment of Massachusetts Volunteer Infantry 1863-1865:* Boston; Boston Book Company, 1894

Gilchrist, Marianne McLeod, "The Shaw Family of Staten Island: Elizabeth Gaskell's American Friends, *The Gaskell Society Journal*, v. IX, 1995, pp. 1-12

Hanson, Chadwick, The 54th Massachusetts Volunteer Black Infantry as a Subject for American Artists, *The Massachusetts Review*, v. XVI, Autumn 1975, pp. 759

Hine, Darlene Clark, ed. Black Women in America: An Historical Encyclopedia, Brooklyn, Carlson Publishing Inc., 1993

Kirstein, Lincoln, *Lay This Laurel*: New York; Eakins Press, 1973

Lucas, Justin, "Le Salon Des Salons (1898): Art et Critique," *Revue Encyclopedique*, No. 252, 2 Juillet 1898, pp. 600-603

The Monument to Robert Gould Shaw: Its Inception, Completion and Unveiling 1865-1897, Boston; Houghton Mifflin and Co., 1897

Marcus, Lois Goldreich, "The Shaw Memorial by Augustus Saint-Gaudens: A History Painting in Bronze," *Winterthur Portfolio*, v. XIV, No. 1, pp 1-24

Nichols, Rose Standish, "Familiar Letters of Augustus Saint-Gaudens," McClure's Magazine, v. XXXI, October, 1908, No. 6, pp. 603-616

Saint-Gaudens, Homer, ed. *The Reminiscences of Augustus Saint-Gaudens*, New York; The Century Co., 1913

Thompson, Joann Marie, *The Art and Architecture of the Pan-American Exposition, Buffalo, New York, 1901.* Ph.D. dissertation, Rutgers University, New Brunswick, N.J., 1980

Wade, Hugh Mason, A Brief History of Cornish, 1763-1974, Hanover; University Press of New England, 1976, p.38

Walton, W., *Exposition Universelle, 1900: The Chefs-D'oeuvre*, Philadelphia; George Barrie & Son, Publishers, 1900

Wilkinson, Burke, *Uncommon Clay: The Life and Works of Augustus Saint-Gaudens*, San Diego; Harcourt Brace Jovanovich, 1985

Wilson, Joseph T., *The Black Phalanx: A History of the Negro Soldiers of the United States in the Wars of 1775-1812, 1861-65*, Hartford; American Publishing Company, 1888

Yacavone, Donald, ed., *A Voice of Thunder: The Civil War Letters of George E. Stephens*, Urbana; University of Illinois Press, 1996

MANUSCRIPTS

Albright Knox Gallery, Buffalo, New York, Museum Archives

Archives of American Art, Smithsonian Institution, Washington, D.C., various collections

Dartmouth College, Hanover, New Hampshire, Special Collections, The Papers of Augustus Saint-Gaudens and The Papers of the Trustees of the Saint-Gaudens Memorial

Library of Congress, Washington, D.C., Charles Follen McKim Papers

Massachusetts Historical Society, Boston, Massachusetts, Luis F. Emilio Collection and Atkinson Family Papers

The Museum of Fine Arts, Boston, Massachusetts, Museum Archives, Papers of General Loring

Schlesinger Library, Radcliffe College, Cambridge, Massachusetts, Emerson-Nichols Papers

Syracuse University, Syracuse, New York, Special Collections, The Papers of James Earle Fraser

ACKNOWLEDGEMENTS

Many individuals assisted with their time, suggestions, and research on this project. I would especially like to thank the following for their help: the staff at Special Collections, Dartmouth College Library, William Loos, Buffalo Central Library, Rare Books & Manuscript Division, the staff at Special Collections, Syracuse University Library, Catherine L. Mason, Erie County Historical Society, Janice Lurie, Albright Knox Art Gallery, Maureen Melton, Boston Museum of Fine Arts, Ann Wheeler, National Cowboy Hall of Fame, Robert Jaccaud, Dartmouth College Library, Judith N. Lund, New Bedford Whaling Museum, Susan Greendyke Lachevre, Massachusetts Art Commission, Elizabeth Ajemian, Joyce Schiller, Diane P. Fischer, Elizabeth Krawczyk, James Percoco, Lawrence Nowlan, Bridgid Sullivan, Carol Warner, Clifford Crane, and Don Wickman.

Pencil sketches of ideas for
the Shaw Memorial by
Augustus Saint-Gaudens,
1882-1883.

All historic photograhs by
Dewitt Clinton Ward,
Saint-Gaudens National
Historic Site.

Pencil sketches of ideas for the Shaw Memorial by Augustus Saint-Gaudens, 1882-1883.

Above: Exploring the idea of incorporating a woman holding a child in the design.

All historic photograhs by Dewitt Clinton Ward, Saint-Gaudens National Historic Site.

First version, October 1896.

Third version, April 1898.

Second version, May 1897.

Fourth version, April 1900.

A COMMEMORATION

The American journey has not ended.
America is never accomplished. America is always still to build.
—Archibald MacLeish

And the crown is as bright o'er the sable
brows as over the golden hair.
—George H. Boker

L ike those mighty oaks that from tiny acorns grow, national epics often stem from events that are small in their own right, and it may take years for their transcendent message to be fully grasped by the national imagination. Such was the case of the assault on Fort Wagner, South Carolina, July 18, 1863, by the Fifty-Fourth Massachusetts Volunteers under the command of Colonel Robert Gould Shaw. Although the attack failed and the regiment quickly withdrew after sustaining heavy casualties, the gallantry of its African American troops and the heroic death of its youthful Boston Brahmin commanding officer received immediate notice in the press and set in motion reverberations that have been felt to this day. The Fifty-Fourth's symbolic value had, in fact, been foreordained. If not the first, it was the preeminent all-black regiment, albeit officered mostly by whites, to be formed in the Civil War and was intended to show the effectiveness of blacks as fighting men and, more broadly, to prove their manhood. The regiment became a metaphor for emancipation born in a baptism of fire. Then, from an early commemoration by James Russell Lowell, "Memoriae Positum, R.G.S., 1863" published in the *Atlantic Monthly* (January 1864)[1] through its most recent in the film *Glory*[2] released in 1989, the march of its symbolic portrayal has moved from an orig-

Architectural drawing by Henry N. Richardson.
Courtesy Houghton Library, Harvard University, Cambridge, Mass.

After the unveiling, May 31, 1897.

inally limited Bostonian and Union context to its ultimate recognition as the basis of an American epic, embodying our fundamental values and continuing aspirations of equality and liberty.

Despite the widespread contemporary reportage of the event for its propaganda effect and its sporadic precursory commemorations, the continuing march of the epic was not assured until the sculptor Augustus Saint-Gaudens captured the essence of its meaning with aesthetic power and moral conviction in his memorial to Robert Gould Shaw and the men of the Fifty-Fourth (see illustration). Since its dedication one hundred years ago on Decoration (Memorial) Day 1897, this unforgettably moving bronze monument has given the epic both permanence and prominence in its Boston Common location near one of the cradles of the American Republic. Without this constantly viewed reminder, the significance of the Fifty-Fourth might gradually have faded as a memory of an ever more distant war. Moreover, this monument was singular in its recognition of the contributions made by African American soldiers and of blacks and whites fighting together in support of national values. It would be hard to exaggerate the importance of the Shaw Memorial and its role in the epic making process. From the time of its unveiling, the centennial of which we are now celebrating in 1997, the monument has sustained our common vision of the epic. Future echoes of the theme were to hark back to this intense sculptural expression, reflecting upon it and drawing inspiration from it, as much as from the wartime event itself. In this sense, the artist Saint-Gaudens has served as the Homer of the Fifty-Fourth and of the Civil War.

The march of the Fifty-Fourth as epic had actually begun before the end of the war. The event began its transfiguration into poetry not long after the dramatic Fort Wagner assault, and its retelling in the arts has continued to this day. The epic has had its ebb and flow of interest, as did the history of the event itself. As time passed, reportage yielded to historiography, and aesthetic expression was manifested in an ever-expanding range of art forms and genres—poetry, essay, prints, sculpture, photographs, film and television. There was also interplay among them—poem harking back to poem, monument displaying verse, essay explaining sculpture, monument inspiring poem, poem prefacing symphonic piece, sculpture glossing film, and criticism entwined with all. Immediate reactions came during the war, and occasional commemorations followed over the next few years. The animating vision in the march of the epic came with the dedication of the Shaw Memorial by Augustus Saint-Gaudens in 1897 and the outpouring of expression which surrounded it. A later series of variations on the theme came with the Civil War Centennial in the early 1960s, and yet another in the late 1980s and 90s, spurred on by another revival of interest in the war and in the field of African American history, culminating with *Glory* and *The Civil War* series. Although commonly, if not always, the product of cultural elites, versions of the epic have succeeded in broadening their appeal to reach mass popular audiences.

Perhaps the first voice sounding an epic tone for the Regiment was that of a private in Company A. The sentiments expressed here in a song, published early in 1863 in the *Boston Transcript,* preceded the engagement in battle but were later justified by the heroism at Fort Wagner.

McClellan went to Richmond with two hundred thousand brave:
He said, keep back the niggers,' and the Union he would save.
Little Mac he had his way, still the Union is in tears:
Now they call for the help of the colored volunteers.

                                    ❮

So rally, boys, rally, let us never mind the past:
We had a hard road to travel, but our day is coming fast;
For God is for the right, and we have no need to fear:
The Union must be saved by the colored volunteer.
Chorus—Oh! Give us a flag all free without a slave,
We'll fight to defend It as our fathers did so brave:
The gallant Comp'ny A will make the rebels dance,
And we'll stand by the Union, if we only have a chance.[3]

This would seem to indicate that enlisted soldiers from the Regiment's rank and file also believed in the special mission of the Fifty-Fourth and that they accepted the challenge. By their acts they hoped to help to save the day for the Union and to join in the mainstream of history with those who had defended it in the past.

In the aftermath of battle, the meanings and ironies of the sacrifice were expressed in many forms and on varying cultural levels. One of the most cogent depictions is found in a poem written shortly after the assault on Fort Wagner by George H. Boker.

> "They buried him with his niggers!"
>   Together they fought and died
> There was room for them all where they laid him
>   (The grave was deep and wide)
> For his beauty and youth and valor,
>   Their patience and love and pain;
> And at the last day together
>   They shall be found again.
>
>   ☾
>
> "They buried him with his niggers!"
>   But the glorious souls set free
> Are leading the van of the army
>   That fights for liberty
> Brothers in death, in glory
>   The same palm branches bear;
> And the crown is as bright o'er the sable brows
>   As over the golden hair. [4]

They were together in life, in death, and in glory.

Pictorial views of the assault on Fort Wagner, either in sketches or photographs, illustrated contemporary accounts in newspapers and magazines. Wood engravings of the attack and a portrait of Shaw along with an obituary, "The Late Colonel Shaw," appeared in *Harper's Weekly*. Other pictorials were issued as separate prints of the type popularized by Currier and Ives as were many photographic portraits of the Fifty-Fourth's officers and men—some of which were later reproduced in Luis Emilio's official regimental history.[5] One of these was of Sergeant William H. Carney of Company C who gained fame, and ultimately the Congressional Medal of Honor, for his successful efforts to save the national colors during the battle. In the photograph, used as frontispiece for the history, he is shown holding the flag with a caption identifying it as the one he saved at Wagner and quoting Carney, "The old flag never touched the ground, boys." This story inspired a sculptor, Truman Howe Bartlett, to inquire about Carney's exploits, saying that he "would make a splendid subject for a statuette." Colonel Hallowell replied with a verbal description: "Sergt. Carney was an African, of I should think full blood; of very limited education, but very intelligent; bright face, lips and nose (comparatively) finely cut, head rather round, skin very dark, height about five feet eight inches, not very athletic or muscular; had lived in New Bedford, Mass., for many years."

If a "statuette" was ever completed on the basis of this description, it obviously would not have been an accurate personal likeness. It can be assumed that most contemporary illustrations conveyed a certain symbolic representation of truth rather than historical accuracy.[6]

That Shaw himself would come to personify the gallantry of the Regiment was to be expected. Not only was he its commander, but coming as he did from an exalted station in society, he received a high level of attention and respect for his sacrifice. His heroic death was held as both a personal and family loss and as a moral contribution of Boston and Harvard to the preservation of the Union and the redemption of the colored race. The epic process in this vein enlisted the best New England literary talent, including Ralph Waldo Emerson and James Russell Lowell who were personal friends of the Shaw family. Lowell's "Memoriae Positum, R.G.S., 1863" was the first major poem to focus on the nobility of Shaw's death in the prime of his youth and its transcendent significance for the nation. While the tone is intensely personal, the ode ends with a salute to the land which produced such dedication.

> Brave, good, and true,
> I see him stand before me now.
>
> ☾
>
> Right in the van,
> On the red rampart's slippery swell,
> With heart that beat a charge, he fell
> Forward, as fits a man;
> But the high soul burns on to light men's feet
> Where death for noble ends makes dying sweet;
>
> ☾
>
> His life's expense
> Hath won for him coeval youth
> With immaculate prime of Truth;
>
> ☾
>
> Ah, when the fight is won,
> Dear Land, whom triflers now make bold to scorn
> (Thee! from whose forehead Earth awaits her morn!)
> How nobler shall the sun
> Flame in the sky, how braver breathe the air,
> That thou bred'st children who for thee could dare
> And die as thine have done![7]

In sculpture, a bust of Colonel Shaw was completed before the war's end by Edmonia Lewis. She was born of a Negro father and a Chippewa mother, and had received formal training as a sculptor in Boston through the influence of the abolitionist leader William Lloyd Garrison. The bust of Shaw was praised by critics and, as reproduced in plaster copies, achieved a modest commercial success. It also launched a successful career for the artist who went on to work in Rome and to produce a number of studies on Indian themes as well as one of a slave man and woman rejoicing at the news of emancipation.[8]

Although planning for a great monument commemorating both Shaw's personal gallantry and the symbolic heroism of the Fifty-Fourth began in late 1865, the final memorial, brilliantly executed by the New York sculptor Augustus Saint-Gaudens, the foremost commemorative sculptor of his day, was not completed and dedicated until 1897. The original fund-raising committee, chaired by governor John Andrew himself, included Senator Charles Sumner and the poet Henry Wadsworth Longfellow. By 1883 the fund had reached more than $16,000, and Augustus Saint-Gaudens was contracted to undertake the project in the following year. The artist devoted parts of the next twelve years to completion of what was to become his greatest work. The noted architect Charles Follen McKim designed the pedestal, benches, and stone frame into which the bronze sculpture was placed. Saint-Gaudens excused his long delay on the project "on the ground that a sculptor's work endures for so long that it is next to a crime for him to neglect to do everything that lies in his power to execute a result that will not be a disgrace. There is something extraordinarily irritating, when it is not ludicrous, in a bad statue. It is plastered up before the world to stick and stick for centuries, while man and nations pass away. A poor picture goes into the garret, books are forgotten, but the bronze remains . . ."[9]

The life-sized monument is a simple metaphoric statement of what the war was ultimately about, white and black together under arms marching into battle to preserve the Union, to emancipate the slaves, and to lead the nation, as Lincoln put it, to a new birth of freedom. At the center of the sculpture, Colonel Shaw is portrayed on horseback, drawn sword in hand, riding at the side of a group of his colored soldiers who are marching in columns four abreast with shouldered muskets and colors rising well above the level of the men. At the far right a drummer boy is in the lead, and above them all floats an angel on her divine mission urging them forward. The overall impression made by the figures is one of realism. Even the angel seems lifelike. While each figure is notably individual in appearance and expression, together they convey a sense of resolve and common purpose, marching to fulfill their destiny. Based on photographs and other portraits, the likeness of Shaw is historically accurate. For the drummer boy and soldiers Saint-Gaudens relied on models chosen from Negroes available in New York City to serve as types that he wished to portray, as he did in the case of the angel. The net result is striking in its verisimilitude, a forceful and well-crafted expression of the monument's symbolic meaning.

The memorial is also replete with verbal messages. Cast within the bronze between the troops and the angel's arm is the inscription *Omnia relinquit servare rempublicam* (He leaves everything behind to save the republic), motto of the Society of the Cincinnati, a fraternal, patriotic organization formed by the regular officers at the end of the Revolutionary War. Below, on the pedestal, is the dedication to Robert Gould Shaw, Colonel of the Fifty-Fourth Massachusetts Infantry, followed by a stanza from the 1864 Lowell poem "Right in the van." Other inscriptions are on the back of the monument, including the homage of Harvard's President Charles W. Eliot.

Artistically, the monument is within its genre the greatest American achievement of its day and arguably the finest piece of memorial sculpture ever produced in this country. Augustus Saint-Gaudens masterfully captured the spirit of his times and projected it in sculpted form. Sculpture, especially on a large commemorative scale, came to enhance our public space, as did parks, squares, government buildings, libraries, museums, and concert halls in the period from 1876 to 1917 recalled as the American Renaissance.[11] It was the era of the "City Beautiful" movement when one international exposition followed another, and the need was felt to express national identity and pride symbolically through works of art and architecture. The grand traditions of the Italian Renaissance provided models, and Saint-Gaudens like many of his contemporary artists had been strongly influenced by them during years of apprenticeship in Rome and study at the Ecole des Beaux-Arts in Paris. Standard elements of Renaissance iconography including the equestrian presentation of Shaw and even the form of a guiding angel were well suited to this monument and were the types of images that the viewing public had come to expect. Saint-Gaudens' collaborator Charles McKim also held to the values of the Renaissance, in his execution of this memorial, in much of his architectural work, and in his founding of the American Academy of Rome.

Aesthetically, the monument's impact has been profound from the outset. Writing in the *Century Magazine* shortly after the dedication ceremonies in 1897, William A. Coffin described the work in all of its detail and concluded, "How unified and complete it is! With what force is the general effect brought to one, making him feel the grandeur of the whole! . . . No poet's dream of heroism, glory, or devotion . . . could be realized in material form as this is . . . this beautiful work of art."[12] Another contemporary critic Lorado Taft, as noted by a later art historian Albert Boime, thought it was "one of the most impressive monuments of modern time," and compared Saint-Gaudens's treatment of the upraised, shouldered muskets with that of lances in Velasquez's "Surrender at Breda." He was especially struck by the realistic sense of marching conveyed by the bronze figures, " The movement of this great composition is extraordinary. We almost hear the roll of the drums and the shuffle of heavy shoes. It makes the day of that brave departure very real again." It is "the fit expression of America's new-born patriotism."[13] A few years later, a black art historian, Freeman Murray, praised the work of Saint-Gaudens for "instinct with taste and technical mastery, yet sublime in its expressiveness and mighty in its moving power."[14]

Nearly a century later its power to evoke an emotional response is undiminished. In a recent biography of Saint-Gaudens, Burke Wilkinson describes the Shaw Memorial as a "Symphony in Bronze." . . . There is so much variety to it, from the delicate bas-relief of the hovering angel to the high relief of many of the marching men, to the full statue-in-the-round quality of the Colonel and his charger, that no other musical analogy would be accurate. To carry the comparison one step further . . . musically speaking the instruction under which the sculptor composed hls symphony was *nobilmente* . . .[15] The combining of the techniques of full round, high relief and bas-relief, may also be thought of as the artist's separate treatment of Shaw as portrait, the soldiers as realistic but representative types, and the angel as allegory—the closer to historical accuracy, the fuller the sculptural form the same tripartite division may be seen to represent yet another separation—of underlying purpose, Shaw's devotion to duty and sense of noblesse oblige, the patriotic and self-fulfilling sense of manhood on the part of the troops, and the angel's expression of divine message.

The symbolic representation was most apt and the commemoration complete. It all needed to be there: Shaw, his men, and the sense of mission. An equestrian statue of Shaw alone, as Saint-Gaudens had originally conceived the monument, would have been pretentious. Unlike General Sherman, another of the sculptor's subjects, the young colonel was not sufficiently heroic in his own right, and his military contribution to the war had been slight. Shaw's family was correct in insisting that the memorial should include the men of the Fifty-Fourth, since the sacrifice at Fort Wagner had meaning only in martyrdom of blacks and whites fighting and dying for one another. While the figure of Shaw on his horse is central to the composition, he is there to lead his men as liberators of their race. They are mutually dependent. The beckoning angel is needed to complete the metaphoric message that the march of the two together toward equality must continue, that victory still lies ahead, that the new birth of freedom envisioned by Lincoln has yet to be achieved.

Long anticipated, well planned, and dramatically executed, the dedication of the Shaw Memorial finally came about on Decoration Day, May 31, 1897. It amounted to no less than a gala civic celebration engaging the elite of Boston and veterans of the war in a final consecration of Shaw as local hero and of the Fifty-Fourth Regiment as the ultimate symbol of the state's Union patriotism and moral virtue. The monument would stand as a perpetual reminder of this sacrifice, becoming a part of Bostonian elite lore. The ceremonies began on Boston Common with the unveiling of the statue and a few words by Governor Roger Wolcott, followed by a twenty-one gun salute and a military parade including sixty-five veterans of the Fifty-Fourth which passed before the reviewing stand constructed on the steps of the Statehouse across the street from the monument.[16] Here they marched in life for the last time in the same spot that they had earlier with Colonel Shaw on May 28, 1863, when going off to war and under Colonel Hallowell, who had assumed command of the Regiment on Shaw's death, on September 2, 1865, upon their triumphal homecoming. From this day on, their march continued only in the realms of reconstructed image and historical memory.

That night an extended commemoration in honor of the Brotherhood of Man rounded out the festivities. The Boston *Evening Transcript* of June 1 captured the emotional tone of the moment "in the flag-filled, enthusiasm-warmed patriotic and glowing atmosphere of Music Hall, people felt keenly that here was the justification of the old abolition spirit of Massachussetts . . . The scene was full of historic beauty and a deep significance 'Cold Boston' was alive with the fire that is always hot in her heart for righteousness and truth. . . . Battle music had filled the air. Ovation after ovation, applause warm and prolonged had greeted the officers and friends of Colonel Shaw, the sculptor Saint-Gaudens, the memorial committee. The governor and the Negro soldiers of the Fifty-Fourth. . . ." Later, that evening's principal speaker, Booker T. Washington, recalled the crowd's height of exuberance which came as he extolled the bravery of

Sergeant Camey who in turn then rose to his feet and waved the tattered flag which he had carried at Fort Wagner and never allowed to touch the ground. "In dramatic effect I have never seen nor experienced anything that equaled the impression made on the audience. . . . For a good many minutes the audience seemed to entirely lose control of itself and patriotic feeling was at a high pitch.[17] The other major address of the night, given by William James, whose brother Wilkie had served in the Fifty-Fourth, complemented the sentiments offered by Washington. In fact, the two had corresponded earlier in order to coordinate their efforts and avoid duplication.[18] Both, however, developed similar themes, beginning with praise for Shaw and the Fifty-Fourth, then turning to the lessons to be learned from their heroic sacrifice and the goals left to be fulfilled.

In this speech and in an article published two weeks later in *Leslie's Weekly Illustrated,* Booker T. Washington stressed that "it would be hard for any white man to appreciate to what extent the negro race reveres and idolizes the name of Colonel Shaw. Not so much for what he did as for the principle for which he stood . . . Shaw succeeded in making the negro a soldier because he had faith in him as a man." Going beyond personal eulogy, Washington added that "the full measure of the fruit of Fort Wagner and all that this monument stands for will not be realized until every man covered with a black skin shall by patient and natural effort, grow to that height in industry, property, intelligence and moral responsibility, where no man in all our land will be tempted to degrade himself by withholding from his black brother any opportunity which he himself would possess. Until that time comes, the monument will stand for effort, not victory complete. What these heroic souls of the 54th regiment began we must complete . . . in the public school, industrial school, and college . . . most of it must be completed in the effort of the Negro himself . . ." He concluded with a call to realize:

> The slave's chain and the master's alike broken;
> The one curse of the race held both in tether;
> They are rising, all are rising—
> The black and the white together.

White and black, southerner and northerner, and men from all sectors of society would need to work together to achieve the realities of liberty and equality.[19]

For William James the story of Shaw and his Regiment could be read from the monument in "the mingling of elements which the sculptor's genius has brought vividly before the eye. There on foot go the dark outcasts, so true to nature that one can almost hear them breathing as they march . . . warm-blooded champions of a better day for man. There on horseback . . . sits the blue-eyed child of fortune, upon whose happy youth every happy divinity had smiled. Onward they move together, a single resolution kindled in their eyes and animating their otherwise so different frames." For James, Shaw and his comrades showed that Americans of all complexions could fight and die as brothers in order to preserve what he called our American religion, the belief that all men should live in liberty. Slavery had been a perversion of this principle and had to be rooted out. The Shaw monument, then, would serve as a permanent "inciter" to perform similar unselfish public deeds. It would stand as a call for "civic courage," and the lessons of the war were the need to maintain a constant vigil against internal enemies that would undermine the republic.

Democracy was still on trial and depended on the functioning of two common civic habits—respect for the opposition party when it fairly wins elections and an unwillingness to tolerate a breach of the public peace. James concluded by urging his countrymen, "Southern and Northern, brothers hereafter, masters, slaves, and enemies no more . . ." to preserve these heirlooms. Our country would then continue "like the city of promise and the ways of all nations be lit up by its light."[20] Thus, James had gone beyond his initial focus on the monument and the story of Shaw and the Fifty-Fourth to a general call for civic virtue, much as Booker T. Washington had shifted from monument and event to a call for Negro self-improvement. This was a pattern that would be repeated.

The Shaw memorial became more than the centerpiece of this commemoration and of the revived interest in the Fifty-Fourth during the 1890s. It was to transcend community pride of Boston and the symbolism of Harvard's achievement as expressed on the eve of the ceremonies, May 30, 1897, when Major Henry Lee Higginson concluded his commemorative address to students of Harvard University and men of the Grand Army of the Republic with:

> In yonder cloister, on the tablet with his classmates of 1860 is engraved the name of Robert Gould Shaw He will always be an heroic figure for you . . .
>
> Harvard students: whenever you hear of Colonel Shaw, or of any officer or of any man of the 54th Massachusetts Regiment, salute him in the name of Harvard University and Harvard men.[21]

Reactions to the monument varied. Some observers were inspired to praise further the genuine heroism of Shaw and his men, while others contrasted the regiment's sacrifice for human and national values with the corruption or loss of some of these values in later decades. A former army chaplain, James M. Guthrie, for instance, urged "The visitor to Boston, Massachusetts who loves liberty and those who died for it, should not fail to see among its many shrines in that city, the monument erected to honor the memory of Colonel Robert Shaw (and his gallant regiment). . . . " He also contributed a special poetic tribute to the memory of Sergeant W. H. Carney entitled "The Old Flag Never Touched the Ground."

> March on, Black soldiers, in the van, free Negroes of the North,
> And each one prove yourself a man—a man of equal worth
> With any in the ranks of those who boast that they are White
> And for this reason are your foes: show them that you can fight.[22]

Of a very different tone was the sonnet "Robert Gould Shaw" by the leading Negro poet of his times, Paul Laurence Dunbar, who had in earlier, more optimistic days sung the praises of Negro troops in his ode to "The Colored Soldiers" which ended:

> And their deeds shall find record
> In the registry of Fame,
> For their blood has cleansed completely
> Every blot of Slavery's shame.

By 1900, however, Dunbar had become bitterly disillusioned. While his admiration for Shaw remained intense, he concluded in the poem "Robert Gould Shaw" that his sacrifice had been in vain, that the ideals for which he had died were no longer honored in the present.

> Why was it that the thunder voice of Fate
> > Should call thee, studious, from the classic groves,
> > Where calm-eyed Pallas with still footstep roves,
> And charge thee seek the turmoil of the state?
> What bade thee hear the voice and rise elate,
> > Leave home and kindred and thy spicy loaves,
> > To lead th' unfettered and despised droves
> To manhood's home thunder at the gate?
> Far better the slow blaze of Learning's light
> > The cool and quiet of her dearer fane,
> Than this hot terror of a hopeless fight
> > This cold endurance of the final pain—
> Since thou and those who died for right
> > Have died, the Present teaches, but in vain![23]

Yet another sort of interpretation was offered in 1900 by the poet William Vaughn Moody in "An Ode in Time of Hesitation" after seeing and reflecting upon the meaning of the monument. For him, the memorial inspired a sweeping condemnation of America's Philippine policy which stood in contradiction to the ideals expressed by Shaw and his men. Moody looked back on Shaw and the Fifty-Fourth as redeemers of our national purpose and honor. They followed the just and righteous path toward liberty where death and glory met

> To show all peoples that our shame is done,
> That once more we are clean and spirit-whole . . .

The validity of their sacrifice and our national honor, however, were again being put to the test by those who urged our country to subject yet other peoples—in the Pacific and in Cuba—this time to a colonial form of enslavement. Moody concluded with a challenge to our leadership to reject this course and to remain true to the ideals embodied in the Shaw monument.

> —O ye who lead,
> Take heed!
> Blindness we may forgive, but baseness we will smite.[24]

The American composer Charles Ives added another artistic dimension to the epic of Shaw and the Fifty-Fourth by juxtaposing music with poetry. His poem stands independently, preceding the score, rather than serving as a lyric; yet the images of both are coordinated to telling effect in their somber mood and plaintive tone. The underlying message of both is that of shared human purpose which Ives treats mournfully but with a sense of past and still-to-becontinued heroic resolve. First written about 1910, the piece was revised some twenty years later, and it was published in 1935 as "The Saint-Gaudens in Boston Common (Col. Shaw and his Colored Regiment)," the opening movement of his "orchestral set" *Three Places in New England.* The added dissonance of the new version undoubtedly added to its haunting air of mystery.[25]

The poem and the music are moving in their content and symbolism, as well as their emotional impact.

> Moving—Marching—Faces of Souls!
> Marked with generations of pain,
> Part-freers of a Destiny,
> Slowly, restlessly—swaying us on with you
> Toward other Freedom!
>
> «
>
> Above and beyond that compelling mass
> Rises the drum-beat of the common heart
> In the silence of a strange and
> Sounding afterglow
> Moving—Marching—Faces of Souls!

In the verses and the music Shaw and his phantom troops move ponderously and resolutely forward in their muffled march, shrouded in the darkness of death, relieved only by an afterglow of hope. They continue the march toward other freedom and sway us to fall in beside them. The slow incessant drumbeat cadence of the march and of the common heart are one. It carries all forward beyond a fleeting crescendo of struggle, moving toward future fulfillment, as if following Saint-Gaudens's beckoning angel. The music and the poem end where they began, "Moving—Marching—Faces of Souls!"

If representations of Shaw and the Fifty-Fourth done in poetry, sculpture, oratory, music, and journalism were in large measure responsible for the continued march of the epic, the longterm underpinnings for its historiographical development came from Captain Luis Emilio's *History of the Fifty-Fourth Regiment of Massachusetts Volunteer Infantry, 1863-1865.* Although Emilio, as commander of Company E, had been an eye-witness and participant through much of the regiment's life, he based his regimental history additionally on an extensive compilation of contemporary letters, government reports, and journals as well as on conversations with other veterans of the unit. In 1890, the History's publishers praised the work for being more than just another regimental history and one that would be of special interest to the new generation of the race from which the Fifty-Fourth was recruited. Its style was straightforward and its "plain narrative of the soldierly achievements of this black regiment is better evidence of the manly qualities of the race than volumes of rhetoric and panegyric could convey." They also thought it would appeal to the general public, for men of the regiment shared the patriotism and courage that characterized citizen soldiers in general. It was a typical regiment and yet it occupied a prominent position in representing the political policy of emancipation. The publishers felt fully justified in adding to the title the epithet, "A Brave Black Regiment." Later the Officers' Association of the Regiment adopted the work as its authorized history, and a second revised and corrected edition appeared in 1894. This work and other historical writings were to have an increasing impact on the epic-building process in its subsequent periods of revived development in the latter half of the twentieth century.

At mid-century, following decades of lapsed interest in Shaw and the Fifty-Fourth, two remarkably stark and beautiful poems, John Berryman's "Boston Common A Meditation upon the Hero" and Robert Lowell's "For the Union Dead (Relinquunt Omnia Servare Rem Publicam),"[26] served as a prelude to the epic's revival which followed in the years of the Civil War Centennial (1961-1965) and beyond. Both works draw inspiration from direct observation of the Saint-Gaudens monument and from reading the essay on it, on Shaw, and on the theme of civic courage by William James. Both poems, however, are written in dark tones reflecting a bitter disillusionment with the present, as if evoking the past in search of an elusive redemption. Both poets laud the past heroism of Shaw and his men but find their virtue anachronistic in face of the horrors of World War II and the cold detachment of contemporary society. For them the monument was less an "inciter" to continue the march or to pursue civic courage and more a symbol of an America gone by and now gone astray. If Moody had written ". . . in Time of Hesitation," Berryman and Lowell were writing seemingly in a time of anxiety and despair. The two poets were nonetheless inspired by the monument, moving from it to their social analysis, aesthetic expression, and musings of gloom.

"Boston Common" is the earlier, the longer, and the more cryptic of the two works. The poem centers on a visual and symbolic contrast between the heroic monument of the past and the "casual man" of the present, a dispossessed derelict who was sleeping beneath "the impressive genitals of the bronze charger."

> Immortal heroes in a marble frame
> Who broke their bodies on Fort Wagner's walls,
> Robert Gould Shaw astride, and his
> Negroes without name, who followed, who fell,
> Screaming or calm, wet or cold, sick or oblivious.
> Who now cares how? here they are in their prime,—
>
> ☾
>
> Imperishable march below
> The mounted man below the Angel, and
> Under, the casual man, the possible hero . . .

The casual man lying passively "in shapeless failure" represented for Berryman "the last straw of contemporary thought." Now a "terrible shape, defeated and marvelous," the man under the stallion "is our whole hope . . . and our despair, the heart of the Future beating." He is in essence the statistical man of a non-caring society. Yet he may have been an unsung hero of forgotten "civic soul." Memorializing of heroes depended on "accidents of history." Honor should go to all who give, not to the selected few. For Berryman, the monument stands as a "frame of hope" and as a "dramatic bivouac" drawing attention to the unheeded casual man. Together in bronze and in life they stand to be reconciled in worship and in love. All of this is treated in a transcendent human sense, a recognition of the brotherhood of man, but the racial question is ignored. Had the derelict been black, the poem would have had an added message.[27]

Robert Lowell in "For the Union Dead" was still more pessimistic. While the "monument sticks like a fishbone in the city's throat," whatever message it may have had is ignored by a society in which "a savage servility slides by on grease." The poem is highly local in scope, a lament for the city of Boston, overwhelmed by the mechanized ugliness of the modern world, a world that itself seems much closer to disaster. He notes that there are no statues for World War II and refers to a photographic image of "Hiroshima boiling." The meaning of the Civil War seems to live on only in the Yankee stiffness of Shaw's personal image and in Lowell's nostalgia stripped of sentimentality. Saint-Gaudens's "Civil War relief" is now imperiled by the construction of a garage under Boston Common, where once "William James could almost hear the Bronze Negroes breath."

Its Colonel is as lean
as a compass-needle.

He has an angry wren-like vigilance,
a greyhound's gentle tautness,
he seems to wince at pleasure
and suffocate for privacy.

He is out of bounds now. He rejoices in man's lonely,
peculiar power to choose life and die—
when he leads his black soldiers to death,
he cannot bend his back.

On a thousand small town New England greens,
the old white churches hold their air
of sparse, sincere rebellion, frayed flags
quilt the graveyards of the Grand Army of the Republic

The stone statues of the abstract Union Soldier
grow slimmer and younger each year—
wasp-waisted, they doze over muskets
and muse through their sideburns . . .

Lowell's reverie remains focused on New England and on the Union. There is no sense of national reconciliation here, and the ideals of the past have yielded to the nightmares of the present As for race, he contrasts Colonel Shaw's "bell-checked Negro infantry" with the present-day "drained faces of Negro school-children . . ." rising "like balloons" on his television set.[28] Lowell, in fact, saw "For the Union Dead" as an "abolitionist poem" and later said, at the height of the civil rights struggle in 1964, that he lamented the loss of the old abolitionist spirit: "The terrible injustice, in the past and in the present, of the American treatment of the Negro is of the greatest urgency to me as a man and as a writer."[29] For Lowell, however, the monument seemingly embodied no hope, no living march, and no epic. It was a fading reminder of a dying past in the midst of a harsh, chaotic present increasingly bereft of traditional values. And yet, behind it all there was a glimmer of hope which stuck like a fishbone in the throat of the poet, provoking him to write one of his greatest works.

"For the Union Dead" later prompted American studies scholar Steven Axelrod to chart the poem's cultural pedigree.[30] For him, the poem expands upon the details of earlier works, and responds to their themes, and with it "Robert Lowell completes the task begun by James Russell Lowell, William Vaughn Moody and John Berryman of transforming Shaw and the Fifty-Fourth Massachusetts from obscure Civil War heroes into national symbols, in order to dramatize an increasingly bleak moral situation." Writing in the early 1970s, Axelrod also refers briefly to the Saint-Gaudens' monument and to the William James dedication speech. Axelrod echoes Lowell's pessimism of a decade earlier in his contention that "These poets have been engaged in an extended losing battle with history, which has ended in moral defeat, leaving us only their artistic consolation."[31] While Axelrod was right in seeing the poems of Robert Lowell and his predecessors as part of a process, moving from local obscurity to national symbolism, he was mistaken in his conclusions. First, these poems were not in their own right sufficiently compelling or of broad enough appeal to complete the transformation to a national epic. Robert Lowell, however gifted a poet, was writing as yet another Bostonian and Harvard man—James Russell Lowell, Moody and Berryman were also all Harvard men—whose work added to the process of epic building but far from completed it. Second, Axelrod erred in seeing this as a completed process, which had ended with the closure of its moral significance. And third, he failed to grasp the overriding centrality of the Saint-Gaudens monument, which by its continued, commanding presence on the Boston Common stood as a beacon to steer the process through and well beyond the pessimism of Berryman, Lowell, and the period of the late 1960s and 1970s. Despite these shortcomings, Axelrod's article serves as one of the earliest and most important interpretations on the artistic continuity of the theme.

In the 1960s, however, the more positive and forward-looking continuations in the march of epic building came not in poetry but in other genres: history and biography. The Civil War Centennial and the most turbulent years of the civil rights movement coincided to spark an explosion of historical reassessments of the war in all of its complexities. In this, special attention was given to the role played by the Negro in the war and his failure to achieve the full promise of equality in the decades that followed. The war, black history, and the symbolic sacrifice of Shaw and the Fifty-Fourth offered themes which were mutually supportive and which gradually became more central to a general discourse on America's past and present.

On the particular nexus of the war, blacks, and the Fifty-Fourth, no one has been more sustained and forceful in his contribution to academic history than Princeton's James M. McPherson. His pioneering work, *The Negro's Civil War*, was first published in the same year of the Voting Rights Bill of 1965 and the close of the Centennial period. Quite contrary to the bleak prospects for humanity expressed earlier by Berryman and Lowell, the '60s were, as McPherson recalled when the book was reissued twenty five years later, "... a time of optimism in race relations much like the heady days of 1865, ..." a time of looking forward to a bright future. Moreover, the demands of Negroes for freedom and equality made in the 1960s were again as fresh and relevant as they had been a century earlier. Those were the days in which Americans were spellbound when President Lyndon Johnson echoed Martin Luther King's prophecy that, we shall overcome. The *Negro's Civil War* was the first book to express the war's history largely in the words of the blacks themselves, and the exploits of the Fifty-Fourth at Fort Wagner provided the principal focus of the chapter "Negro Soldiers Prove Themselves in Battle, 1863."[32] In the years following 1965, McPherson returned repeatedly to the theme of Shaw and his black regiment—in *Marching Toward Freedom: The Negro in the Civil War 1861-1867* (1967), in his "Foreword" to the reprint of Luis Emilio's *A Brave Regiment* (1969), in *Battle Cry of Freedom* (1988), in his "Foreword" to James Henry Gooding's letters, *On the Altar of Freedom* (1991).[33] Yet, despite his efforts and the ever-increasing flow of scholarship concerned with the African American experience in slavery and in the Civil War and its aftermath, McPherson admitted that there remained a general lack of awareness in the story of Shaw and the Fifty-Fourth until the public's interest was aroused by the film *Glory* in 1990. While raising questions in a review article, "The 'Glory' Story," about the conflict of historical accuracy and poetic or metaphoric truth, he stressed the potential of the film to reach millions of viewers, correcting earlier filmic distortions.[34]

Peter Burchard, previously most noted as an illustrator and writer of books for young people, made the greatest single contribution of the 1960s to the epic with his *One Gallant Rush: Robert Gould Shaw and His Brave Black Regiment*. Not only was this the first book-length biography of Shaw but it influenced subsequent writing on Shaw and his regiment both directly and through the film *Glory*, the screenplay of which was based largely on Burchard's book.[35] Burchard was first drawn to the theme while writing a piece for young readers on an earlier attack on Fort Wagner.[36] In *One Gallant Rush*, his interpretation is in the traditional vein of Shaw and the Fifty-Fourth as exemplars of the free Negro's ability to fight. Shaw had ultimately embraced the Negro's cause as his own personal crusade, and in dying with many of his men shared their heroic fate. The title is taken from Frederick Douglass' assessment of the Regiment's prospects: "The iron gate of our prison stands half open, one gallant rush . . . will fling it wide." Burchard ends the work with his own assessment of what Shaw meant to his compatriots:

> To New Englanders of his own time, Shaw, in his youthful Victorian innocence, seemed a kind of saint. In the last few months of his life, in his latter days and final hours, he had drawn on his forefathers' deep convictions and sense of duty and his own devotion to the cause which had rekindled the imaginations of New England's poets and scholars, preachers and teachers and practical men. In his last hours, Shaw had indeed caught fire and to those who had devoted their lives to the breaking of the back of the American shame, his death was an evening and a dawn.[37]

The centrality of the Saint-Gaudens memorial to the continuation of the epic was reaffirmed in a collaborative effort directed by Lincoln Kirstein, poet, cultural activist, publisher, and founder of the New York City Ballet, who had a long-standing interest in the contribution of blacks to the arts in America. Kirstein also felt a personal affinity with Colonel Shaw. He had, like Shaw, been raised in a civic-minded family in Boston and had roomed with a descendant of Shaw's at Harvard. The project resulted in *Lay This Laurel: An Album on the Saint-Gaudens Memorial on Boston Common, Honoring Black and White Men Together Who Served the Union Cause with Robert Gould Shaw and Died with Him July 18, 1863* a striking book, rich in its blending of visual and verbal imagery, and beautifully produced by Kirstein's Eakins Press.[38]

Here, Richard Benson's poignant photographic study, comprising sixteen duo-tone plates of the monument, interspersed with epigraphs by Emily Dickinson, Frederick Douglass, Walt Whitman, and Abraham Lincoln, among others, is linked to Lincoln Kirstein's essay on the art of Saint-Gaudens and the historical events behind it. Their intent was to make the Shaw memorial available to "young Americans, patriots, art lovers, and others" beyond its fixed site in Boston, for it was a deserving "focus for pilgrimage, a civic shrine, a national reminder" and "an incomparable work of sculpture." This was art in service of patria and racial reconciliation. The critical times for black Americans in the 1960s and '70s called for a broader recognition of the work aesthetically and in its transcendent message. Kirstein further explained his intent:

> It is especially to black artists—writers, composers, painters, sculptors, and choreographers—that this essay is aimed, for past any taint of racial chauvinism, Saint-Gaudens's work demonstrates how one vastly gifted, socially responsible white artist, operating on intractable material with an objective eye and resolute control over hand and eye, persisted through long years, resisting the easy impatience of his patrons, to achieve an individual representation worthy of the gigantic event the sculpture commemorates.
>
> Of all of Saint-Gaudens's work, it is the monument to Robert Gould Shaw and his soldiers of the Fifty-Fourth Regiment of Massachusetts Volunteers which magnetizes the most passionate admiration and repays the closest attention.[39]

Kirstein's essay then traces the story of Shaw and of the Fifty-Fourth as well as that of the Saint-Gaudens monument. Not only does the work stress the role of the blacks and the joint nature of their sacrifice along with whites, but the book includes the first commemorative listing of the black enlisted men who fell at Fort Wagner.

Benson's photographs were done at a low point in the history of the monument's care and preservation ca 1970. The figures are streaked with corrosion and the background matted with soot. Colonel Shaw's sabre is broken off within inches of the hilt, and even the stone frame is in ill-repair. Yet the power and message of the memorial are inescapable, and Kirstein concludes:

> Robert Shaw and his men march onward in the grave mutations of their modeling, moving towards some undefined, perhaps undefinable futurity in ominous ways less predictable than that which faced them when they went forth in the flesh more than a century ago.
>
> The exquisite justice of the placement of the mounted colonel whose leadership was as natural as breath itself, amidst the marching volunteers is on a level of translucent legibility and sudden reality unequaled in Western art. One may search many centuries in public places to discover a civic memorial so perfectly appropriate, achieved with such strength, subtlety, and finesse.[40]

A decade later in 1981 the civic consciousness of Boston was aroused to save the monument from possible collapse and destruction through the initiative of Boston's Friends of the Public Garden. Harvard's Fogg Museum made a study, funds were raised ($200,000), and restoration began. Through an article in *Time,* the "American Scene—In Boston Aid and Comfort for 'The Shaw'," Otto Friedrich brought the plight of the memorial to national attention. Henry Lee, president of the Friends of the Public Garden, whose great grandfather had been on the original Shaw memorial committee, was one of the restoration project's prime movers. The monument was renewed and in a sense completed by the chiseled addition of the names of all of the black enlisted men who had fallen at Fort Wagner. David Mehegan noted in the *Boston Globe Magazine* that its restoration showed the almost magical way in which a work of art allied with stirring events and ideas can rally diverse people and move them to action. Henry Lee added, "The monument honors black and white men who served their common cause. Our hope was that in drawing attention to this, we could do a little bit toward healing some of our present conflicts." As for the future of "The Shaw," an endowment fund was also raised to assure its proper care and maintenance in perpetuity.[41] Thus restored and improved, the monument was ready for the mass distribution of its visual impact that would be provided by the film *Glory*.

In 1989 the release of the film *Glory* brought the epic of Shaw and the Fifty-Fourth to its fullest and most dramatic expression to date. In the film and subsequent video version the epic was to gain a mass national audience, spanning all geographic regions and all levels of culture from elite to popular, which had been left unreached by its earlier forms. In 1990 Ken Burns made television history, with his miniseries *Civil War,* which became the most highly acclaimed documentary ever produced. Thus the media of film and television worked in concert to raise popular interest in the Civil War to new heights and to capture the national imagination with the historical reality and symbolic significance of the sacrifice at Fort Wagner. The epic could now be widely seen as the embodiment of our prime and continuing values of unity, equality, and freedom.

Once an idea for a film has germinated, its realization is a collaborative affair from the outset. In most cases, as with *Glory,* it is impossible to give a preponderance of credit to one individual. The idea in this case came from Lincoln Kirstein, who had been committed to popularizing the epic of Shaw and particularly of his black soldiers since his Eakins Press project *Lay This Laurel*. It was this book, along with Peter Burchard's biography of Shaw, *One Gallant Rush*, and the letters of Shaw himself, that served as the basis for the screenplay. Kirstein then kindled scriptwriter Kevin Jarre's interest in the project. Jarre

Matthew Broderick as *Col. Shaw*.
Photo courtesy TriStar Films.

Denzel Washington as *Trip*.
Photo courtesy TriStar Films.

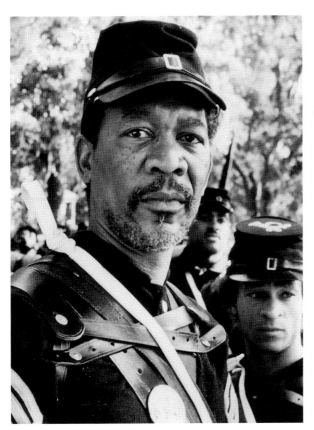

Morgan Freeman as *Rawlins*.
Photo courtesy TriStar Films.

in turn presented a draft script to Freddie Fields, who then became point man for the project and producer of the film. The early agreement of Matthew Broderick to play Shaw helped, and Field's success in drastically cutting cost projections, mainly through the use of non-professional battle "re-enactors," finally convinced Tri-Star's chairman Jeff Sagansky to undertake the making of *Glory*. Edward Zwick, another Harvard man with prior admiration for Shaw and the Fifty-Fourth, was chosen to direct and James Horner to compose the musical score. The film was generally well cast and many of its on-and off-screen participants obviously felt a deep commitment to the film and to the underlying message of the epic which it dramatized.[42]

Like the Saint-Gaudens memorial, *Glory* is basically an ensemble piece presented on different levels of historical and metaphoric reality. At its core, the film is the story of the Fifty-Fourth Massachusetts Regiment. Its purpose, its formation, its training, its combat history through the gallant failure at Fort Wagner, and its transcendent message. It correctly describes the origin of the unit as the product of Boston's abolitionist fervor and portrays Colonel Shaw as its enabling agent. While Shaw serves both as the film's central character and as its narrator—by means of voiced-over excerpts from his wartime letters—he in no way overwhelms it. As in the monument, Shaw (played by Matthew Broderick) is treated in the equivalent of full round, not only as commander of the regiment but again as the only historically genuine personage in the film, aside from the minor figures of his family, Governor Andrew and Frederick Douglass.[43]

The four principal black characters—Trip (Denzel Washington), Rawlins (Morgan Freeman), Sharts (Jihmi Kennedy), and Searls (Andre Braugher)—are all fictional. They are highly individualized but are still types drawn to illustrate both the broad divergence of background of the soldiers and the wide range of attitudes they held concerning white and black society, the war, and the purpose of the Fifty-Fourth regiment. Their treatment in the film corresponds to the high relief used by Saint-Gaudens to depict the varying types he chose to represent with the bronze soldiers of his monument.

The ultimate level of metaphoric reality conveyed by the sculptor in his bas-relief angel is expressed in the film through James Horner's musical score which hovers just beyond the vision of the screen, as if urging the troops forward on their historic mission. Both the music and the angel serve as constant reminders to the viewer of this sense of yet-to-be-fulfilled mission which is central to their respective artistic formulations. Moreover, each representation was well suited to the audience of its day. Sculpted angels were as commonplace in the 1890s as stirring film scores in the 1990s. All three of the elements which were essentially linked to continue the march of the epic in Saint-Gaudens were thus recast, however inadvertently, in the film—Shaw, driven at first by duty and at the end by personal conviction; the black soldiers fighting for their manhood and national participation; and a divine expression of moral imperative—and again, as was the case in the monument, the closer to historical accuracy, the fuller the artistic representation.

In addition to fine acting and the compelling storyline, excellence in other elements behind the scenes—set design, costumes, sound, special effects, and especially the skilled direction of Edward Zwick—assured the superior quality of *Glory*'s production. Moreover, an unusually pervasive musical score by James Horner combined with *Glory*'s striking visual presentation, grounded in Freddi Francis's brilliantly realistic, sharp-focused color photography, to make an uncommonly strong impact in the viewer, demanding of him an emotional as well as intellectual response. Throughout the film the motif of the march, musically and visually, is centrally geared to eliciting this response. Symbolic of order, discipline, training, mutual dependence, and dedication to mission the march motif builds from boot camp to parade leaving Boston, then from the regiment's first battle success in the woods of South Carolina to the initiation of the assault on Fort Wagner. The drumbeat cadence and whistle of the fifes draw the viewer forward along with the columns of marching black troops in their blue uniforms. The pace accelerates into quick time, and the soldiers follow Shaw and the flags of Massachusetts and the United States into battle. At the moment of Shaw's death, the full orchestra and the Boys' Choir of Harlem break into a Carmina-Burana-like exhortation which continues until the battle scene's abrupt conclusion.

At the conclusion of the film, following the brilliantly conceived and executed battle scenes of the climactic assault on Fort Wagner, the scene jumps to the mass burial of the Union dead where symbolically the bodies of Colonel Shaw and the rebellious Trip are thrown together into a common grave on the beach in front of the fort. The scene then shifts abruptly again to a full-frontal view of the Saint-Gaudens monument on Boston Common where Shaw and his men, no longer white and black, but immortalized in bronze, march on to a reprise of the score's march motif—at first heroic, and then plaintive—as a background against which are shown the film's initial credits. The rest of the crawl of credits is then seen against a black field while the musical score continues the march as if fading into the distance. Moreover, the musical handling of the entire march motif, rising to battle crescendo and then falling to reprise and fade out, is like an extended, more blatantly heroic, less dissonant, and demystified version of the Charles Ives, "Saint-Gaudens in Boston Common."[44] Thus, in its concluding moments, the film harkens back to the memorial as its final reference point, welding together the epic of Shaw and the Fifty-Fourth as history and art. The appearance of the monument serves a recapitulative gloss for the film just seen. The aesthetic and emotional impact of this is extraordinary.

Viewing it may encourage members of its audience to explore other versions of the epic, to read the long succession of poems from James Russell Lowell to Robert Lowell, to listen to Charles Ives' *Three Places in New England,* or to study the historical and biographical accounts written for adults or younger readers, or to see first hand, or in photographs, Saint-Gaudens' memorial with its undiminished power to inspire.

Ludwig Lauerhass, Jr.
University of California
Los Angeles

NOTES

Photograph. Bronze memorial to Colonel Robert Gould Shaw and the men and officers of the Fifty-Fourth Massachusetts Volunteer Infantry Regiment by Augustus Saint Gaudens, framed by Charles F. McKim, Boston Common, dedicated 1897. Photograph with permission of the Boston Public Library, Fine Arts Division, photographer and date unknown.

Epigraphs. Archibald MacLeish quoted in Daniel J Boorstin, *The Americans: The Democratic Experience* (New York: Random House, 1973), p 523. George H. Boker, "They buried him with his riggers'," in James M. Guthrie, *Camp-fires of the Afro-American or, The Colored Man as Patriot* (Cincinnati, Ohio: W.H. Ferguson, [1899?]), pp. 467-468.

1. [James Russell Lowell], "Memoriae, R.G.S., 1863," *Atlantic Monthly*, 13, no. 75 (January 1864), pp. 88-90.
2. Kevin Jarre, "Glory," script rewrite by Eduard Zwick and Marshall Herskovitz (Los Angeles, Ca: Glory Productions, 1988); originally issued as the film *Glory* ([Los Angeles] Tri-Star Productions, 1989); reissued on laser disc *Glory* ([Los Angeles] RCA, Columbia Pictures, Home Video, 1990).
3. William Wells Brown, *The Negro in the American Rebellion: His Heroism and His Fidelity.* (Boston, Ma: Lee and Shepard, 1867; New York, NY: Johnson Reprint, 1968), pp. 157-158.
4. Ibid pp 202-203.
5. *New York Times,* July 27, 1863, p. 1; *Harpers Weekly,* vol. 7, nos. 345, 346 (August 8, 15, 1863), pp. 509-510, 525-526; "The Gallant Charge of the Fifty-Fourth Massachusetts (Colored) Regiment," in *Currier and Ives, Chronicle of America*, edited by John Lowell Pratt (Maplewood, N.J.: Hammond, 1968), p. 165; Luis F. Emilio, *History of the Fifty-Fourth*. Regiment of Massachusetts Volunteer Infantry, 1863-1865, second edition, revised and corrected (Boston, Ma:, Boston Book Company, 1897) reprinted as *A Brave Black Regiment*, with a foreword by James M. McPherson (New York, NY: Arno Press, 1969)
6. Brown, *The Negro in the American Rebellion,* pp. 210-211.
7. [James Russell Lowell], "Memoriae Positum," pp. 88-90.
8. On Edmonia Lewis see Albert Boime, The Art of Exclusion: Representing Blacks in the Nineteenth Century (Washington, DC: Smithsonian Institution Press, 1990), pp. 161-171, which reproduces a photograph of her bust of Shaw; *The Booker T. Washington Papers* (Urbana, Ill: University of Illinois Press, 1975) vol.4, p 43, n.3.
9. Edward Atkinson, "History of the Shaw Monument by the Treasurer of the Fund," in *The Monument to Robert Gould Shaw, Its Inception, Completion, and Unveiling, 1865-1897* (Boston Houghton, Mifflin, and Company, 1897), pp. 7-13, and "The Shaw Memorial and the Sculptor St. Gaudens, I. The History of the Monument," *Century Magazine,* vol. 54, no. 2 (June 1897), pp 176-178; Burke Wilkinson, *Uncommon Clay: The Life and Works of Augustus Saint-Gaudens,* (New York, NY: Harcourt, Brace, Jovanovich, 1985), pp. 279-288, The Reminiscences of Augustus Saint-Gaudens, edited by Homer Saint-Gaudens (New York, NY: The Century Company, 1913), vol. 2, pp. 78-84.
10. An early description and evaluation of the monument is William A. Coffin, "The Shaw Memorial and the Sculptor St. Gaudens, 11. The Sculptor St. Gaudens. "*Century Magazine,* vol. 54, no. 2 (June 1897), pp. 179-193. For recent treatments see Wilkinson, *Uncommon Clay, pp. 274-288;* Louise Hall Tharp, Saint Gaudens and the Gilded Era (Boston: Little, Brown and Company, 1969), pp. 267-283; Boime, *Art of Exclusion,* pp. 199-219. Boime's interpretation is especially interesting as it rests largely on a discussion of the work of a nineteenth-century black art historian, Freeman Henry Morris Murray, *Emancipation and the Freed in American Sculpture: A Study in Interpretation* (Washington, DC: the author, 1916).
11. Brooklyn Museum, *The American Renaissance, 1876-1917* (New York, NY: Pantheon Books, 1979).
12. Coffin, "The Sculptor St. Gaudens," p. 184.
13. Lorado Taft, *The History of American Sculpture* (New York, NY: Macmillan, 1903), pp. 302-304, 363, as quoted in Boime, *Art of Exclusion,* pp. 204-205.
14. Quoted in Boime, *Art of Exclusion, p.* 204. Boime concludes that Murray's personal attachment to the Shaw monument led him to see it as "the ideal memorial, an excellent work of art with the correct' ideological message." Boime has strong reservations about this because of what he contends was Saint Gaudens's underlying racism, pp. 199-219.
15. Wilkinson, *Uncommon Clay, p. 274.*
16. Ibid, p. 286, "Unveiling the Shaw Monument, May 31, 1897," *in The Monument to Robert Gould,* pp 37-49.
17. Boston. Evening Transcript, June 1, 1897 quoted in *The Booker T. Washington Papers,* vol. 1, pp 109-112. See also "Ceremonies at the Music Hall," in *The Monument to Robert Gould Shaw,* pp. 52-96.
18. *The Booker T. Washington Papers,,* vol. 4, pp. 264, 270-272, 285, 292, 295, letters exchanged between Washington and William James regarding their Shaw memorial addresses.

19. Ibid., vol. 1, pp. 106- 109, vol. 4, pp. 300-302.
20. William James, "Robert Gould Shaw," in *Memories and Studies* (New York Longman's Green, and Co., 1917), pp 40-61. His description of Shaw as a "blue-eyed child of fortune." (p. 40) may have been slightly incorrect. The copy of The *Monument to Robert Gould Shaw* owned by the University of California Davis Library had originally been presented to Mrs. Francis G. Shaw, Robert's mother. Among the handwritten corrections in this copy, one appearing in the address given by Major Henry Lee Higginson corrects his text which refers to Shaw's "merry *blue* eyes" to "light hazel."
21. Henry Lee Higgins, "Address," in *The Monument to Robert Gould Shaw,* pp. 21,36.
22. James M. Guthrie, *Campfires of the Afro-American,* pp. 468-473.
23. *The Collected Poetry of Paul Laurence Dunbar,* ed. by Joan M. Brixton (Charlottesville University of Virginia Press, [1993]), pp. 50-52, 221.
24. William Vaughn Moody, "An Ode in Time of Hesitation," *Atlantic Monthly,* vol. 85, no. 511 (May 1900), pp. 593-598.
25. Charles E. Ives, *Three Places in New England* (Boston: C.C. Birchard, 1935); *Charles Ives—Memos,* edited by John Kirkpatrick (New York: W.W. Norton 1972, pp. 85-87. Elliot Carter in *Charles Ives Remembered. An Oral History,* edited by Vivian Perlis (New Haven Yale University Press, 1974), p. 138. For a recorded version, consult Howard Hanson conducting the Eastman-Rochester Orchestra, Charles Ives, *Three Places in New England* [New York, NY: Polygram "Mercury,] Records).
26. John Berryman, "Boston Common: A Meditation upon a Hero," in *The Dispossessed* (New York: William Sloan Associates, 1948), pp. 63-68, Robert Lowell, "For the Union Dead, Relinquunt Omnia Servare Rem Publicam,'" in *Life Studies and For the Union Dead* (New York, NY: Farrar, Straus, and Giroux, 1964), pp. 70-72.
27. Berryman, "Boston Common," pp. 63-68.
28. Lowell, "For the Union Dead," pp. 70-72.
29. Robert Lowell as quoted in lan Hamilton, *Robert Lowell: A Biography (New* York: Random House, 1982), p. 281.
30. Steven Axelrod, "Colonel Shaw in American Poetry: For the Union Dead and its Precursors," *American Quarterly,* vol. 24, no. 4 (October 1972), pp. 523-537.
31. Ibid., pp. 523, 530-531, 537.
32. James M. McPherson, *The Negro's Civil War: How American Blacks Felt and Acted During the War for the Union* (New York, NY: Ballantine Books 1991; first published New York Pantheon Books, 1965), pp xi-xvi I, 191-196.
33. James M. McPherson, *Marching Toward Freedom: The Negro in the Civil War,* 1861-1867 (New York: Alfred A. Knopf, 1967), "Foreword" in Luis Emilio, *Brave Black Regiment, Battle Cry of Freedom: The Civil War Era* (New York, NY: Oxford University Press, 1988); and "Foreword" in Gooding, *On the Altar of Freedom.*
34. McPherson, *The Negro's Civil War,* pp. xii-xiii, James M. McPherson, "The 'Glory' Story," *New Republic,* vol. 202 (January 8, 1 5, 1 990), pp. 22-23, 26-27.
35. Peter Burchard, *One Gallant Rush: Robert Gould Shaw and His Brave Black Regiment* (New York St. Martins, 1965) The paperback edition, issued in 1989, has added to the cover: *Glory . . . The True Historical Saga,* Dramatized in the Major Motion Picture *Glory.*
36. Peter Burchard, telephone conversation, December 3, 1993.
37. Burchard, One Gallant Rush, pp. xii, 147.
38. Richard Benson and Lincoln Kirstein, *Lay This Laurel: an Album on the Saint-Gaudens Memorial on Boston Common: Honoring Black and White Men Together Who Served the Union Cause with Robert Gould Shaw and Died with Him July 18, 1863* (New York: Eakins Press, 1973), unpaged, see "Acknowledgments" at end, telephone conversation with Leslie Katz, editor of the project for the Eakins Press, December 9, 1993. In a recent study Nicholas Fox Weber treats Kirstein as one of our cultural patron saints in *Patron Saints: Five Rebels Who Opened America to a New Art, 1928-194 ~* (New York, NY: Knopf, 1992).
39. Ibid., unpaged, see the first two pages of Kirstein's essay.
40 . Ibid., unpaged, see the Benson photographs and the last and the 95th to the last pages of the Kirstein essay.
41. Otto Friedrich, "American Scene—In Boston: Aid and Comfort for 'The Shaw,'" Time, vol. 117, no. 14 (April 6, 1981), pp. 4-5; David Mehegan, "For These Union Dead," *Boston Globe Magazine* (September 5, 1982), pp. 10-11, 29, 32-33.
42. Benson and Kirstein, *Lay This Laurel,* and Burchard, *One Gallant Rush.* The sequence of involvement in the project comes from telephone conversations with Burchard, December 3, 1993; Leslie Katz, December 9, 1993; Edward Zwick, January 5, 1994; Freddie Fields, March 9, 1994.
43. Jarre, "Glory [Script]," *Glory* [film]; Glory [laser disc].
44. Ives, *Three Places in New England*

CONSERVATION OF THE SHAW MEMORIAL

The conservation history of the *Robert Gould Shaw Memorial* spans almost exactly one century, dating from the first major conservation campaign in 1901 when the plaster, upon return from exhibition in Paris, was prepared for exhibit at the Pan-American Exposition in Buffalo, to the conservation effort now in progress to prepare the Shaw for exhibit in the National Gallery of Art in Washington D.C. This current effort was initially born of a growing concern over the physical deterioration of the Shaw by years of exposure to ambient conditions in its outdoor exhibit location at Saint-Gaudens National Historic Site in Cornish, New Hampshire. Though providing shelter from direct rain and snow, the roofed three-sided structure in which the Shaw was displayed provided no protection against damaging extremes of both temperature and relative humidity, and no protection against abrasive and corrosive airborne particulates and gaseous pollutants destructive to the plaster over time.

CONDITION

Decorative Surface:

Various campaigns of localized surface treatments and cosmetic interventions over the years had resulted in distractingly patchy overall appearance.

When the surface of the Shaw was examined by conservators from the National Park Service and from Daedalus, Inc. shortly before the present conservation project began, flaking of the metal leaf coating was apparent in several areas on the front, most notably on the proper right trouser cuff of the drummer, and the side and bottom of the drum. Small blisters and fissures were visible throughout the surface.

Plaster:

Numerous small surface cracks and superficial chips were observed and recorded before the plaster was dismantled. Stress cracks were pronounced along the front of the base in four locations, and across the rear legs and the right front leg of the horse.

In general, when the sculpture was dismantled, the plaster was found to be in stable condition. The past conservation campaigns, which included consolidation of the surface with Acryloid B-72, and gilding with metal composition leaf followed by toning layers and protective coatings of lacquer and wax, served to protect the plaster from exposure to the elements. However, when disassembly began, the plaster in some areas such as the upper background section containing the angel relief, were found to be friable and porous.

Dismantling and removal of overfill along the section joins revealed extensive previous repair to damaged edges of the sections and many layers of overfill that had been applied to disguise misalignments in previous installations.

Background relief section showing fill (textured) along damaged join line.

Armature:

Of greatest concern was the deteriorated condition of the armature support. The 1992 Condition Report, prepared by the Center for Conservation and Technical Studies noted visible rust on exposed areas of the iron wire armature elements on Shaw's spur and on the horse's tail, mane, reins, bridle and bit, on the front of the sculpture. In the back, rusting of exposed iron and staining of plaster indicated active corrosion. The increase in volume of the armature due to corrosion, had caused chipping, cracking and detachment of plaster both in contact with, and adjacent to, rusting iron elements. Some of the exposed thinner wire elements had broken.

The Shaw was again examined in 1995 by Conservator Clifford Craine of Daedalus, Inc. who noted that the exposed wood elements of the armature structure were soft and spongy with rot in some places, and in many areas, the wood was no longer in direct contact with the plaster, due to displacement of the plaster in response to expansion and contraction of the wood and fiber constituents over time with changes in relative humidity and temperature.

Mr. Craine's assessment of the overall stability of the sculpture at the time of his examination is as follows:

> The actual present condition of the sculpture is in reality difficult to ascertain with any degree of certainty. This is because the front of the cast is covered with a restored decorative surface, and the back of the cast is covered by the added external armature, and a concrete wall. However, the presence of many small cracks in the surface of the sculpture was noted as early as the 1981 Fogg conservation treatment record, and again in the 1989 Dennis and Craine memo. Pronounced cracking was noted along some of the seams, especially in the upper right hand corner and on the horizontal surfaces of the base. Losses of plaster surface adjacent to rusting wire armatures in the horse's mane and elsewhere have also required on-going conservation treatment. *These observations, coupled with the finding that many of the components of the 1959 external armature are not well adhered, suggest that the structural stability of the sculpture in its present environment and its present configuration is questionable. It seems prudent to assume that if conditions are unchanged, deterioration will only continue.*[1]

In pursuit of long-range preservation of this unique and important work of art, the current project to make a mold and replicate the plaster in bronze for continued display on-site, was inaugurated in 1996 by the Trustees of the Saint-Gaudens Memorial and the National Park Service. Arrangements were made to loan the original plaster art work to the National Gallery of Art in Washington D.C. for conservation and exhibition where it can be safely displayed and enjoyed by thousands of visitors.

Shelter for the Shaw Memorial,
Saint-Gaudens NHS, Cornish, NH, 1959-1996.

Understanding of the present condition of the *Shaw Memorial* in the context of its complex treatment history was necessary to develop an appropriate conservation approach for all phases of the project: disassembly, mold-making, re-assembly, and final surface treatment. Clifford Craine of Daedalus Art Conservation Inc., Cambridge, MA, was contracted by the National Park Service and the National Gallery of Art as the project chief conservator for all phases, including reassembly and surface treatment at the National Gallery in Washington D.C. Mr. Craine had previous first-hand experience with the *Shaw Memorial* when he worked on the last major conservation campaign in the early 1980s as a staff member of the Center for Conservation and Technical Studies.

Conservation History:

The plaster cast was executed by Saint-Gaudens in his New York studio at about the same time that the bronze cast of the Memorial was being completed for installation on the Boston Common in 1897. He intended the plaster cast to be shown along with other examples of his work, at various exhibit venues. The plaster Shaw version differs from the bronze, primarily in the detail of the background bas-relief angel, which Saint-Gaudens continued to develop artistically until 1900. The plaster version was intended for exhibit, specifically at the 1898 Paris Salon *Societe Nationale des Beaux Arts* to be followed by exhibit in the 1900 *Exposition Universelle* in Paris, and finally, the 1901 *Pan American Exposition in Buffalo*. The design of the sculpture in about twenty-one sectional units allowed it to be broken down for shipment and reassembled in various exhibit venues. Each move, however, required installing support armature in the back, filling and finishing of section joins as well as an overall final surface treatment to achieve the appearance of a solid sculptural unit.

Installation at the National Gallery will mark the ninth episode of complete dismantling and reassembly of the plaster cast in its history, and the tenth episode of complete surface treatment. The current effort seeks to develop a surface treatment plan that will be consistent with the last appearance personally directed and endorsed by Saint-Gaudens, as substantiated by archival documentation, and physical evidence obtained by scientific examination of surface samples.

SURFACE TREATMENT HISTORY: DOCUMENTARY EVIDENCE

Treatment as Directed by Saint-Gaudens:

In January 1898, the plaster cast was packed at the New York studio by art packers from the Boston Museum of Fine Arts and shipped to Paris. The cast was initially reassembled at Saint-Gaudens' Paris Studio in April, then dismantled again and transported to the site of the 1898 Salon.[2] We presume that Saint-Gaudens directed reassembly and cosmetic finishing of the Memorial, but little is known of the surface treatment or appearance other than that which can be extrapolated from inspection of a photogravure image that exists showing the Memorial on display at the Salon.

When the Memorial was next moved in 1900 at the Grand Palais for the *Exposition Universelle*, it is clear that Saint-Gaudens was actively involved in the surface treatment of the reassembled plaster of William A. Coffin, Artistic Director of American Art for the Exposition, who wrote that *"The Shaw had been colored. It was all set up and it was 'finished,' but Saint-Gaudens told me that it was too dark and he was having it all done over with a tint and rub-down to make it lighter."*[3] *". . . he is having the Shaw colored bronze . . ."* noted Mrs. Saint-Gaudens' sister in May 1900.[4]

In 1901, the *Shaw Memorial* was shipped to Buffalo, New York for exhibit in the Pan American Exposition. Documentation in the William A. Coffin papers, that *"after Henry had finished setting it up, the color was matched on the joints and repaired places as closely as possible"* indicates that the surface appearance was unchanged from the Paris Exposition.[5] In fact, a photograph of the opening day of the Pan American Exposition Fine Arts Building shows the *Shaw Memorial* as yet unfinished with section join lines clearly visible.

In March 1905, the cast was to be exhibited at the Inaugural Exhibition of the Buffalo Fine Arts Academy, also known as the Albright Art Gallery, requiring a renewed surface treatment. The process of gold-leaf gilding was interrupted on March 15 when the Shaw was dismantled and moved to a different location within the gallery. The Albright Art Gallery Architect Edward B. Green wrote to Saint-Gaudens in 1905 that *"The flying figure on the Shaw Memorial has been partly covered with gold leaf . . . we stopped the work because the Fine Arts Academy has decided to change the position of the Memorial, and therefore, it must be taken down and moved."*[6]

The plaster was exhibited at the Albright Art Gallery at the end of May, although a final surface treatment was undertaken in July by James Earl Fraser who came to Buffalo as directed by Saint-Gaudens to *"clean, paint and bronze"* the Shaw. This might be interpreted as darkening the bright gold leaf by toning layers.[7]

The *Shaw Memorial* remained on exhibit in the gallery until 1919, at which time it was removed from view by the simple expedient of constructing a new gallery wall in front of it, rather than removing it from the building altogether. It remained out of view for thirty years until 1949, when it was finally dismantled and moved as part of a major gallery renovation of the museum, now known as the Albright-Knox Gallery. Interestingly, the contractor hired to oversee the disassembly was Mr. Joseph Balk, who, as a young man, helped dismantle the Shaw at the close of the Inaugural Exhibit in Buffalo in 1901. The plaster was shipped in sections to Cornish, New Hampshire where it remained in storage until 1959, when the decision was made to exhibit it on the grounds of Saint-Gaudens home and studio under the sponsorship of the Saint-Gaudens Memorial.

Surface Treatment after Saint-Gaudens' Lifetime:

In 1959, the Trustees of the Saint-Gaudens Memorial contracted New York sculptor John Terken, to install and cosmetically repair the Memorial for exhibit. Ten years later, Terken described this project in a letter written to the Saint-Gaudens National Historic Site, *"the original (gold) leaf had sustained much damage and would have been prohibitive to restore. Consequently, I painted it with flat oil paint, first dark, then light. This was followed by varnish and gold powder in stipple effect."* In 1962, as reported in the Claremont (N.H.) *Daily Eagle,* Terken was again contracted to undertake a full restoration of the Memorial because *"Three years of exposure to temperature change and considerable moisture at the Cornish site had resulted in chipping and flaking of the plaster from which the cast is constructed and a general undermining of the material itself was feared."* The restoration consisted of *"sealing of exposed plaster sections and the addition of a 'patina'; a gray-green coloring to resemble weathered bronze, and gilding to add highlights."*[8]

In 1981, the National Park Service embarked on a major conservation campaign to stabilize and restore the Shaw to its original appearance. Nearly twenty years of weathering, and application of maintenance coats of paint since the Terken restoration had resulted in an unattractive chalky appearance. The Center for Conservation and Technical Studies at the Fogg Museum, was contracted to undertake the conservation, and, in 1981, did scientific analysis of the existing layers of surface coatings prior to conservation treatment. In 1982-83, the thick disfiguring restoration paint layers were removed, and the surface regilded with synthetic gold-size, and composition leaf toned with Liquitex emulsion glazes.

In 1986, the Center for Conservation and Technical Studies again treated the plaster to correct discoloration caused by combined effects of weathering, accumulated dirt and pollen deposition. The Shaw was cleaned, reglazed, and inpainted with Liquitex emulsion paint to integrate overly bright areas. From 1986 to 1990, minor structural repairs such as filling plaster losses, consolidating flaking paint, and reattaching recovered loose fragments, were done by the Center for Conservation and Technical Studies, but most of the recent conservation work prior to the current project has been cosmetic in nature.

Surface Treatment: Scientific Examination

Because some plaster rifles, the painted wood sword, and painted metal sword hilt, are detachable pieces, and those elements were missing in the Boston monument, they were used in 1981 by the Center for Conservation and Technical Studies, for replication. When these elements were stripped with solvent in preparation for molding, the conservators noted in the Treatment Report that the following sequence of layers were revealed in the stripping process from the outermost layer, or last surface treatment, to the plaster substrate:

> Green paint
> Turquoise paint
> Darkened or tinted resin
> Metal paint (bronze? Gold?)
> Green paint
> Plaster - wood - metal

It is interesting to compare this observation with microanalytical research findings carried out at the same time by the Center, and subsequently by both the Boston Museum of Fine Arts and the National Gallery of Art.

1981 Analytical Research by the Center for
Conservation and Technical Studies

In 1981, the Center for Conservation and Technical Studies examined six cross sections of surface samples by reflected light microscopy, and one sample was analyzed by scanning electron microscopy with an attached x-ray spectrometer to determine the elements present in the various layers. Pigments in the lower levels were also examined by polarized microscopy.

At least nine distinct layers were identified in all samples, starting with three initial layers common to all: a first layer containing white pigments with chrome yellow and charcoal black which would create a drab olive green color, a second lighter layer also containing synthetic ultramarine blue, creating a pale green, and finally, a third layer with blue, yellow and black, with less white, creating a darker green appearance. Subsequent layers were identified as varnish layers and yellow ground, or mordant layers for metal leaf, with an additional medium-rich dark green layer in which metal leaf, identified as gold with occasional brass leaf identified in layer six and beyond.

The layers associated with the metal leafing (4-6), as well as the lowermost three paint layers were found to be continuous, indicating that the lower layers were in good condition when the metal leaf was applied.

1997 Analytical Research by the Museum of Fine Arts, Boston

With the goal of comparing cross-section layer sequences identified by microscopy to the documentary records describing treatment campaigns, additional analyses were conducted in 1997 by the Research Department of the Boston Museum of Fine Arts. Nine samples were selected from locations likely to contain an uninterrupted surface layer sequence predating the conservation campaign of 1983 when the Memorial was largely stripped of easily removable layers, and the surface regilded with brass leaf and toned.

The samples were examined by reflected light and ultraviolet florescence microscopy. Most of the samples were also analyzed by X-ray florescence in an electron beam microprobe, for general identification of pigments and composition of leaf layers. Isolated layers from selected samples were also analyzed by FTIR microscopy for pigment identification, and by GS/MS for specific medium identification.

The MFA analysis identified six layers common to all samples in sequence from the initial green paint layers directly on the plaster (layers 1 through 3); to a layer of untinted medium (layer 4) which may be a layer of tonal adjustment to the underlying green paint; followed by a layer (layer 5) which appears to be a common ground or mordant for the metal leaf (layer 6).

Many additional layers were found in most of the samples, but no direct evidence of toning layers was seen as a common layer. It is possible that toning may have been done by thin pigmented varnish or shellac glazes, or even by tinted wax, which might not have been durable enough to withstand abrasion by years of cleaning and preparation for new surface treatments. The written research report submitted by the MFA, states that organic colorants may have been used that would not have been readily detectable by the analytical methods used in this research.

1997 Analytical Research by the National Gallery of Art, Washington D.C.

In 1997, a cross-section of a sample taken from the background angel figure of the Shaw before the surface was prepared for molding, was mounted and analyzed by the National Gallery of Art, and shows the full stratigraphy of the Shaw coatings. In the stratigraphic sequence, the latest conservation campaigns from 1983 to 1992, are represented by approximately nine or ten layers that contain combinations of bronze leaf, metallic bronze powder, and dark reddish-brown layers. The restoration campaign of 1959-1962, when the Memorial was installed in Cornish and painted green, is also clearly represented in about six layers, starting with a thick plaster layer probably dating to the reassembly in Cornish by Mr. Terken, and subsequent layers of greenish blue paint. Beneath this the 1905 surface treatment for exhibition at the Inaugural Exposition of the Buffalo Fine Arts Academy is suggested by distinct layers of bole (yellow medium rich layer) and metallic gold leaf, and is consistent with archival evidence. A green layer directly above the plaster corroborates analyses by the MFA and the Center for Conservation and Technical Studies, and evidence of metal leaf or powder in a coat directly above the green paint may suggest the *"tint and a rub-down to make it lighter"* as described by William A. Coffin in Paris in 1900.[9]

The NGA also conducted SEM/EDS analyses of an additional six samples taken from areas least likely to have been disturbed by conservation campaigns before 1983. This was an attempt to gather more information about layer sequence and composition that could be useful in determining the correct historic appearance of the Shaw to guide conservation efforts in the present project.

From the plaster substrate outward, the following common layers were identified. These layers are not always in the actual numerical order of sequential layers identified in each sample, but are numbered here in order to represent shared features among samples.

Representative of the Paris Exhibitions of 1898 and 1900:

    1. Thin grayish green (6 samples)

    2. Light blue (6 samples)

    3. Bluish green (5 samples)

Representative of The Interrupted Campaign of Gilding at The Albright Gallery Exhibition in 1905:

    4. Clear coating or size (5 samples)

    5. Bright yellow (lead chromate, mordant for leafing) (4 samples)

    6. Associated metal layers : gold (3 samples); brass (1 sample)

    7. Clear green (3 samples)

    8. Bright yellow (mordant for leafing) (3 samples)

    9. Associated metal layers: gold (2 samples); brass (1 sample)

    (A discontinuous layer of toned coating or size appears above this layer on 1 sample)

Representative of The Terken Restoration in 1959-62:

    10. Whitish layer (4 samples)

    (Traces of dirt and grime follow on one sample. The green paint used by Terken was probably removed in the 1982 restoration)

Representative of The Fogg Restoration of 1982:

    11. Clear coating of size (5 samples)

    12. Brass metal leaf (5 samples)

    13. Remnants of dark brownish layer of earths and blacks (5 samples)

    14. Coating or size (2 samples)

It is interesting to see that both the MFA and the NGA analyses identify the concurrent use of gold and brass leaf. Sculptural works contemporary to the Shaw, such as the Victory figure of the magnificent *Sherman Monument* and the *Amor Caritas,* demonstrate the artist's use of gilding bronze surfaces to enhance his artistic vision. He was clearly working with this technique at the time of the plaster Shaw's exhibition at the inaugural exhibition of the Albright Gallery in Buffalo. In pursuit of achieving the aesthetic appearance of his gilded bronzes, Saint-Gaudens may have used a combination of the metal leaf available to him to create a gilded surface, over which toning layers could enhance the sculptural quality of the work. Evidence of toning layers over metal leaf appear only sporadically, if at all, in the six sample layer sequences, but do appear in the layer sequence of the two samples taken from the Shaw by the NGA before the disassembly and preparation for molding.

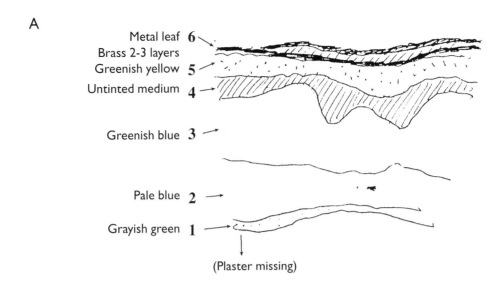

A

Metal leaf **6**
Brass 2-3 layers
Greenish yellow **5**
Untinted medium **4**

Greenish blue **3**

Pale blue **2**

Grayish green **1**

(Plaster missing)

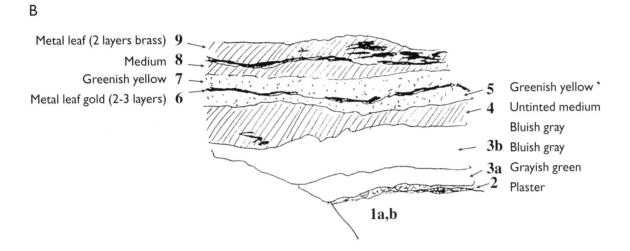

B

Metal leaf (2 layers brass) **9**
Medium **8**
Greenish yellow **7**
Metal leaf gold (2-3 layers) **6**

5 Greenish yellow
4 Untinted medium
Bluish gray
3b Bluish gray
3a Grayish green
2 Plaster

1a,b

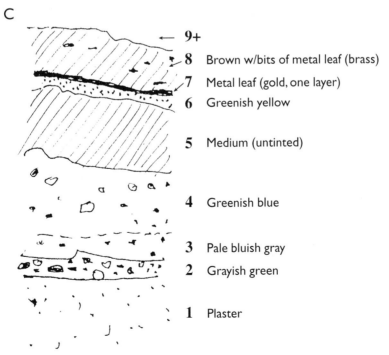

C

← **9+**
8 Brown w/bits of metal leaf (brass)
7 Metal leaf (gold, one layer)
6 Greenish yellow

5 Medium (untinted)

4 Greenish blue

3 Pale bluish gray
2 Grayish green

1 Plaster

A, B, and C. Samples taken from: (A) horse's back leg near rump; (B) back-most soldier's head by ear; and (C) soldier group directly behind horse, behind ear of first soldier.

Based on the array of analyses conducted by the technical laboratories for the National Park Service and the National Gallery of Art, a determination was made in May 1997, to seek a base coating patination that would closely recall the gold leaf with overglazes of umber and translucent green hues as surface scumble. This would to replicate as closely as possible the final treatment of the cast done during the lifetime of the sculptor.

Diagram of Shaw's component sections by Joseph Balk, 1949.

DISASSEMBLY

When the *Shaw Memorial* was taken apart for shipment to Cornish in 1949, contemporary newspaper coverage stated that the Memorial was composed of *"21 pieces that make up the work of art."*[10] In 1992, The Center for Conservation and Technical Studies examined the Shaw, and identified eighteen component sections from evidence of join lines visible on the surface of the sculpture. Joins in the surrounding cornice and side columns make up the rest of the component sections. During the Terken restoration, the plaster sculpture was installed within a three-sided, roofed structure with a concrete back wall. The relief was anchored by means of twisted metal wires held by metal clips set into the mortar between the concrete blocks. No record was made of the number and exact location of the attachments, and visible access to the back of the sculpture was extremely limited due to the proximity of the concrete block wall.

In preparation for disassembly, a radiographic examination of the Shaw was made by Conam Inspection Services of Auburn, Mass. using a radiation source and Structurix X-Ray film from Agfa Division of Bayer Corporation. The examination, directed by Clifford Craine, was made to identify the location of original roman joins, internal armature and method of attachment to the rear wall to assist in developing an appropriate disassembly strategy.

Approximately twenty-four exposures were made, mostly by inserting the sheets of film between the plaster cast and the inside of the concrete wall. The radiographs showed that although the Balk diagram was essentially accurate, many of the original joints in the plaster had been destroyed and/or modified by subsequent campaigns of installation and disassembly. In most instances, pipe was inserted through both ends of the original roman joins, and plastered in place. The original joints of the horse's legs and neck were bridged internally with burlap and pipe, making the horse a single unit. The figure of Shaw was also modified, permanently attaching his proper right leg to his body by means of a pipe through the original roman join. The radiographs also showed that additional iron pipe was used to support the exterior of some of the cast sections at the back of the relief, and also used to attach individual sections together. It was clear from this examination that it would not be possible to dismantle the Shaw in its original component parts.

In addition, a series of misalignments in the back sections containing the angel relief, resulted in a distortion of the cornice line, most noticeable at the egg and dart molding band. These sections were reinforced with metal pipe in the 1959 installation, and because of the thinness of the plaster in the upper backgound area, the misalignment cannot now be safely corrected in the original plaster.

The horse was also incorrectly placed, and tilted forward at an unnatural angle, but because the horse section can be removed from the surrounding sculpture, this feature can be corrected when the cast is reassembled.

The Shaw was dismantled by Daedalus, Inc. in a six-week period in August and September, 1996. The back concrete block wall was dismantled in stages from top to bottom and side to side, as the disassembly of the sculpture progressed.

During the disassembly, the extent of the damage and material loss of section edges through previous installations, was found to be significant, especially in the base, with extensive overfill of adjoining sections. The fill material between sections was removed with chisels and scalpels. Each section was secured with webbing and lifted by means of a block and tackle to a prepared staging area for crating. The sections were moved by Fine Arts Express to the Daedalus conservation laboratory in Boston for conservation and preparation for mold-making.

Dismantling of the Shaw Memorial,
August 1996 by Daedalus, Inc.

Preparation for Mold-Making

At the Daedalus studio in Boston, the 1959 external armature elements were removed, and exposed original plaster was consolidated with dilute applications of acrylic resin. The edges of each section were carefully excavated by chisel and scalpel, and cleaned to the original surface plane. Old, non-historic surface coatings, were removed, and surface losses filled with plaster and textured to integrate them with the original artwork. When possible, old fill material covering the original surface of the sections at the joint lines, was also removed. However, major

Three soldier sections with cleaned and prepared edges.

areas of overfill were present along join lines in the section of the angel relief and in the base, to compensate for the misalignment and forward tilt of the horse. When conservation began to remove this overfill, they found that the original plaster was very abraded, had little or no surface detail, and in some cases, was scored to help attach new plaster skim coats added by Mr. Terken. In these areas, the decision was made to leave the old restoration plaster in place. Cracked and flaking areas were stabilized, and the entire surface was consolidated with Acryloid B-72 followed by Acryloid B-67 and two coats of wax in preparation for mold-making. The completed sections were shipped to Woburn, Massachusetts, for mold-making by Robert Shure of Skylight Studios, Inc.

Mold-Making

The considerable expertise of Robert Shure was absolutely essential throughout the entire project, during which he served as an invaluable link between conservation concerns and the realities of the casting process. Mr. Shure made frequent trips to the Modern Art Foundry to inspect the wax sections before enclosure in investment molds and the final casting in bronze by the lost-wax method. He consulted with the foundry on all aspects of assembly and final finishing.

Mold-making of the component sections was extremely challenging because of deep undercuts and areas of high relief. Because of the status of the plaster as an original artwork, it was not possible to cut the plaster sculpture into functional pieces for the bronze casting process. For example, in terms of mold-making, the section containing the drummer's hands, drumsticks, and straps holding the drum was perhaps the most complex area of the entire sculpture, required fifteen separate mold sections to faithfully capture these three-dimensional features. Registration or rotation marks were made in wax on the plaster wrist of the soldier for incorporation in the rubber mold to mark the correct attachment angle of the hand for the foundry's reference.

The back end of the horse was another challenging feature because the tail wraps around the proper left leg. The tail could not be removed for separate molding, and was too close to the body of the horse at the base to permit application of molding rubber and a plaster jacket, much less room enough to pull the rubber mold from the surface. In these and similar areas of the sculpture containing elements in the round or deeply undercut areas, gates or webs of unsulphonated, oil-based clay were placed in undercuts to contain the liquid molding rubber. A plaster cast was then made of the assembled part molds and trimmed of gates and webs with reference to the original artwork. The trimmed plaster cast was then cut into logical pieces for investing and pouring by the foundry.

A combination of mold rubbers was used according to the surface features of individual sections. Black polysulphide rubber is the most flexible material, and was used for delicate detailed areas because it is easier to pull from complex surfaces. Polyurethane, a stiffer molding rubber, was used in larger, smoother areas like the horse's neck, head and flanks, where a less flexible rubber that would hold its shape was needed. Two coats of Butchers Wax™ were applied to the conserved and consolidated plaster surface as a release agent for the mold rubbers. The wax coatings and the layer of Acryloid B-67 were removed after the molds were completed.

Preparing mold of base.

Plaster cast from part molds of drummer boy hand detail.

Bronze cast being prepared at the
Modern Art Foundry, April 1997.

Drummer boy group showing
clean section edge.

Mold of the horse being prepared.

Wax figure of Shaw in preparation for bronze casting.

Preparation for exhibit in the National Gallery of Art

Because most of the damage to the Shaw over time has been the result of repeated installations, a significant part of this project was the development of an armature system that will permit disassembly with the least possible impact on the integrity of the sculpture. This entails a design system for separate support of individual sections within an encompassing framework. Such a design was developed by the Daedalus, Inc. and will be an integral part of the reinstallation in the National Gallery of Art later this year.

Brigid Sullivan
Chief Conservator
Collections Conservation Branch
Northeast Cultural Resources Center
National Park Service

May 1997

ENDNOTES

1. Craine, Clifford, "Recommendations for The Long Term Preservation of The Shaw Memorial Plaster at Saint-Gaudens NHS," Daedalus, Inc., Cambridge, Massachusetts, April 8, 1995

2. Museum Archives, The Museum of Fine Arts, Boston, Massachusetts. Saint-Gaudens arranged with the Director, Mr. Loring, to have "Chico," the museum's packer, go to the sculptor's New York studio in December, 1897, to pack and ship the Shaw cast to Paris.

3. Dartmouth College, Hanover, New Hampshire, Special Collections, *The Papers of Augustus Saint-Gaudens,* "Reminiscences of Augustus Saint-Gaudens," by William A. Coffin.

4. Schlesinger Library, Radcliffe College, Cambridge, Massachusetts, *Emerson-Nichols Papers,* Letter from Elisabeth Nichols to a relative, May 8, 1900

5. Dartmouth, Letter from William A. Coffin to Augustus Saint-Gaudens, October 19, 1901

6. Ibid, Letter from Edward B. Green to Augustus Saint-Gaudens, March 15, 1905

7. Ibid, Letter from Augustus Saint-Gaudens to Edward B. Green, July 4, 1905

8. Cornish, N.H., Saint-Gaudens National Historic Site, museum archives. Letter from John Terken to James W. Coleman, Jr., September 18, 1969.

9. Dartmouth, "Reminiscences of Augustus Saint-Gaudens," by William A. Coffin

10. Hoffman, Ethel, "At 73, He's Taken Apart His Pan American Jigsaw," *Buffalo Evening News,* March 26, 1949

ACKNOWLEDGEMENTS

We are indebted to the following scientists and conservators who have contributed substantially toward the present conservation project of the Shaw Memorial:

Conservation Scientists

    Richard Newman
    Department of Objects Conservation and Scientific Research
    Museum of Fine Arts, Boston

    1997—Reflected Light Microscopy, FTIR microspectrometry, GC/MS and Electron Microprobe analysis of surface samples. *Museum of Fine Arts, Boston*

    1981—Reflected Light and Polarized Light Microscopy, and SEM analyses with x-ray spectrometer of surface samples. *With Eugene Farrel, Center for Conservation and Technical Studies, Harvard University Museums.*

    Michael Palmer
    Conservation Division
    Scientific Research Department
    National Gallery of Art

    1997—SEM/EDS analysis of surface samples. *National Gallery of Art*

Conservators

    Carol Warner
    National Park Service
    Collections Conservation Branch
    Northeast Cultural Resources Center

    Shelley Sturman
    Conservation Division
    National Gallery of Art

    Henry Lie
    Center for Conservation and Technical Studies
    Harvard University Museums.

Special thanks are extended to **Arthur Beale** of the Museum of Fine Arts for his long, valuable involvement and dedicated advocacy for the conservation of the Shaw Memorial since 1967, when, as a staff member of the Fogg Museum Center for Conservation and Technical Studies, he first recommended preservation measures in a General Collection Survey of Saint-Gaudens National Historic Site.